DEEP ROOTS
LASTING FRUIT

Insights on Faithful Endurance

Contributions By
Shepherds Theological Seminary Faculty

Editor: Thomas Pittman

SHEPHERDS PRESS
www.shepherds.edu

Deep Roots Lasting Fruit:
Insights on Faithful Endurance
Copyright © 2025 Thomas Pittman
All rights reserved.

Shepherds Press
6051 Tryon Road
Cary, NC 27518
www.shepherds.edu

ISBN: 978-1-959454-07-6

Cover and text design by: Amy Cole, JPL Design Solutions

Printed in the United States of America

TABLE OF CONTENTS

INTRODUCTION:
TUTORED BY TREES

Stephen Davey

By the time you finish reading this paragraph, another pastor will have left the ministry. Finish this page, and several more pastors will have packed up their libraries and headed home. Nearly forty vocational church leaders will resign by the end of today, and over two hundred more by the end of the week.

What caused these pastors to walk away from a calling they once passionately desired to fulfill? The reasons might be too long to rehearse, but at the top of the list would be discouragement, isolation, adversity, and spiritual drought.

How can a shepherd survive with joy, thriving in fruitful ministry? I'm not talking about church buildings and budgets—I'm talking about spiritual depth in personal life and pastoral ministry, honoring the Chief Shepherd. The answer may be found in a metaphor often used in Scripture—the picture of a tree, which is used repeatedly throughout the Bible to illustrate the qualities of a godly man.

The psalmist wrote, "Blessed is the man ... [whose] delight is in the law of the LORD, and on his law he meditates day and night. He is *like a tree* planted by streams of water that yields its fruit in its season, and its leaf does not wither" (Ps 1:1–3).

The prophet Jeremiah similarly wrote, "Blessed is the man who trusts in the LORD, whose trust is the LORD. He is *like a tree* planted by water, that sends out its roots by the stream, and does not fear when heat comes, for its leaves remain green, and is not anxious in the year of drought, for it does not cease to bear fruit" (Jer 17:7–8).

Security, stability, strength, productivity, growth, and persever-ance while remaining fruitful and faithful—these are the tree-like characteristics of a man rooted in the rich soil of God's character. That sounds like an invitation to study trees. We might find this invi-tation strange simply because we don't know much about trees, so, without becoming tree-huggers, let's discover how a godly believer—and certainly a church leader—can become *like* a tree.

In childhood, you probably heard that there are not enough trees to sustain life on Earth. It's a proven fact that one mature tree will pro-duce enough oxygen for two people. The trouble is with estimates of four hundred billion trees in existence and one billion being chopped down annually, anxious people have been predicting an apocalyptic threat for generations. Children as young as five years old have been taught that we'd better start planting trees like Johnny Appleseed.

Yale University led the way by launching an aggressive global program to plant one billion trees; the university also conducted the first ever comprehensive survey to determine how many trees there were on the planet. With the help of national forest inventories and newly advanced satellite imaging, a team from the Yale School of Forestry and Environmental Studies spent two years studying all the available data. They were eventually (and embarrassingly) stunned to discover that more than three *trillion* trees were alive and well on planet Earth.[1]

Evidently, we're not running out of trees.

Botanists estimate that at least sixty thousand tree species are alive in our world. But where did the trees—even wood itself—come from? The answer eludes evolutionists, who are forced to admit they can only guess. Evolutionist Elizabeth Stacy from the University of

---

1   Kevin Dennehy, "F&ES Study Reveals There Are Many More Trees Than Previously Believed," *Yale School of the Environment*, September 2, 2015, http://www.environment.yale.edu.

Hawaii conceded, "We know next to nothing about how [trees] got here … we don't know much about how speciation happens in trees."[2]

The fossil record supports the biblical account of creation, revealing that dinosaurs wandered among oak, willow, and magnolia trees. For example, the Wollemi pine tree, often called "the dinosaur tree," was believed to have become extinct approximately 150 million years ago. But, wouldn't you know it, this tree was discovered alive and well in Australia in 1994. When the living Wollemi was compared to fossils presumed to be millions of years old, the tree showed no evolutionary changes.[3]

Perhaps that's because trees didn't *evolve*.

According to Genesis chapter 1, which records events witnessed only by God and angels, God spoke into existence vegetation, plants, and trees on the third day of the creation week. Oxygen, fruit, and foliage were available for God's creation of Earth's animal kingdom and the human race, *the following day!* The timing was sovereignly *perfect!*

Since mankind has studied the tree, we've learned about this amazing creation. We know that each tree exists without any external or internal skeleton to provide support and strength; however, we now know that inside each tree is a robust cell wall, composed of *trillions* of cells that give the tree its strength. The tree is created in a superior rounded fashion allowing it to bend in the wind in all directions, yet it supports a healthy crown of branches and leaves with maximum strength. We've mimicked God's design for trees in our own telephone poles and other devices.

While God created most living things to inhale oxygen and exhale carbon dioxide, trees were created to absorb carbon dioxide and exhale oxygen. Research has also shown that inside each tree is a

---

2   "Tracing the Evolution of Forest Trees," *U.S. National Science Foundation,* November 7, 2014, http://www.nsf.gov.

3   Frank Sherwin, "Trees: an Engineering Wonder," *Institute for Creation Research,* August 31, 2015, http://www.icr.org.

factory where work never ceases. A vascular system in the tree, made up of tube-like systems, draws water up from its roots into the leaves, which then sends nourishment, crafted by the leaves, back down to the roots.

Some trees have been discovered to have defense systems against being overeaten by animals—they can produce a chemical that makes their leaves unsavory. For instance, as a hungry insect salivates on certain elm trees, the tree will chemically reproduce the insect's saliva and emit that chemical into the air. The odor alerts predators who like to eat that insect, prompting them to fly in and feast on those invading creatures.

Even more amazingly, trees communicate amongst themselves through microscopic tubes connecting the roots of different trees. Electrical impulses are constantly passing through the nerve-like cells of these networks from root tip to root tip, broadcasting everything from drought conditions to predator attacks. This sophisticated network below the surface has been nicknamed the "underground internet."[4]

Frankly, the more we discover about the average tree in the backyard or along the street, the more incredible the miracle of its creation. We should remember that trees are not human; they are not alive in the same sense that the Bible refers to animals and humans as having *nephesh*, or a conscious life (Gen 1:24–25). When you chop down a tree, you aren't murdering a self-conscious life. The tree isn't agonizing over the idea of a future life as kitchen cabinets.

The evolutionist, however, by losing the order of God's created priority, wants to extend not only human rights but also mystical powers to trees. That's where the tree-huggers come from.

Not long ago, I was standing in a cashier's line when I noticed a community newspaper reporting on the search for the perfect

---

4   Tom Hennigan, "Talking Trees—Secrets of Plant Communication," *Answers in Genesis*, April 9, 2017, http://www.answersingenesis.org.

spouse. Skimming the article, I read that people seeking a sweetheart don't need the help of friends or dating sites. Instead, they can write a letter to a tree called the Bridegroom's Oak, a five-hundred-year-old oak tree in a German forest that supposedly has the power to bring people together. All you have to do is write a letter describing your desire, and the postal carrier will deliver your letter to that tree. The tree has its own registered address, and letters from around the world arrive *daily*.[5]

That tree can't read your letter, and it won't locate your spouse.

Beyond all this nonsense, trees remain one of God's most marvelous demonstrations of His original creative design. The more we discover about trees, the more they become illustrations of perseverance, stability, and even mentoring. For instance, older scholarship believed that trees competed in a life-or-death struggle for limited light and resources, but current research has shown that trees *assist* each other.

When a young sapling springs up in the shade of a thick forest, older trees *share* nutrients through their roots with the sapling. Older trees even change their root structure to allow space for the roots of a younger tree.[6] God has designed the older trees to assist the younger trees, and that design has an obvious application to us.

Trees not only declare the genius of God but also serve as an illustration for godly believers. God has commissioned older believers to nurture, protect, and teach younger believers who are growing up in the faith—older women teaching younger women (Titus 2), and older men teaching younger men (2 Tim 2).

Perhaps the same antidote to pastors leaving the ministry will be found in this volume, in which older shepherds reach out—root to root, heart to heart—to fellow shepherds serving in their field. The

---

5 Annette Huber, "Bridegroom's Oak," *Atlas Obscura,* November 27, 2017, http://www.atlasobscura.com.

6 Richard Grant, "Do Trees Talk to Each Other?," *Smithsonian Magazine,* March 2018, http://www.smithsonianmag.org.

professors of Shepherds Theological Seminary are publishing this volume with the prayer that it will encourage you to stay the course with joy.

Together, let's act a little more like trees.

1

FEEDING THE ROOTS:
THE KEY TO ENDURANCE

Michael Vlach

I remember a season early in my ministry when I was juggling a lot—teaching multiple courses, preaching weekly, writing, trying to lead my family. The work itself, of course, was meaningful, but I began to notice something subtle. I was growing weary inside. Nothing changed in what I believed or taught. In fact, I was still learning many good and true things. But something was not quite right. And I could function on borrowed strength. But the spiritual gas tank was running low. My relationship with Jesus was not what it should be. The joy that undergirded what I did seemed different. And the Bible had become mostly functional for me.

I learned what many in Christian ministry have experienced. Just "doing" what you're supposed to do is not enough. The work continues, but the soul can become dry. Eventually, shallowness shows, first to yourself and then to others. I also discovered that the only way to endure is to return to the source of life—Jesus. And this takes determination and effort.

When I think about abiding and thriving in Jesus, I have to remind myself that God is seeking relationship. It's about love for Him and then love for others. It's not just about activities, as good as those may be. While I firmly believe that a true believer can never lose his or her salvation, I'm still sobered by Jesus' words in Matthew

7:21–23, where He says that some will come to Him saying, "Lord, Lord," and list their religious accomplishments—only to hear Him reply, "I never knew you; depart from me." Religious work can be done, but if relationship with Jesus is not there, the result is not good.

I'm also drawn to the Bible's imagery of trees and roots. The Bible was written in an agrarian world, where people understood agriculture, seasons, and surviving storms and droughts. So it's no surprise that the idea of being rooted—firmly grounded in the right source— is central throughout Scripture. That's how the Bible speaks of stability, endurance, and a life that bears fruit.

Psalm 1 is a great place to start. It gives the connection between being rooted and prospering: "But his delight is in the law of the Lord, and on his law he meditates day and night. He is like a tree planted by streams of water that yields its fruit in its season, and its leaf does not wither" (Ps 1:2–3). This is what ministry rooted in the Word looks like. Delighting in God's Word continually—day and night. Doing so means being like a tree that is firmly rooted by life-giving water. This kind of life can weather dry months and still stand firm.

In His parable of the soils, Jesus warned of people who respond to the Word with joy but never develop depth. One type of soil produced a plant that shot up quickly. It looked great in the moment. But it had no root. No depth. And so when the sun came out— when pressure and persecution came—it withered. Luke records Jesus saying, "They believe for a while, and in time of temptation fall away" (Luke 8:13). Matthew adds, "When affliction or persecution arises because of the word, immediately he falls away" (Matt 13:21). These words are haunting to me. It is possible to look like one is following Jesus, but time will show that a real connection with Him never existed.

Jesus gave the clearest picture of this reality when He said, "I am the vine, you are the branches" (John 15:5). He is the source of life and without Him we wither and die. Abiding in Him means staying connected in ongoing dependence, communion, and obedience.

"Apart from me you can do nothing," He said. That's not poetic or hyperbolic language—it's a warning. Ministry that is detached from Jesus may look alive for a while, but eventually the branch dries out.

These same principles are echoed in the natural world. Stable trees endure when the winds blow and a storm rolls in. They're not thrown off by dry seasons either when the sun beats down or scorches the ground. That's because the strength of enduring trees isn't in what exists above the ground. It's not about the branches or the leaves or even the trunk. It's in what you can't see. Roots. Long, deep, established. That's where life is drawn from. That's where the stability comes from. Shallow plants dry out. Deep trees endure.

Similarly, pastoral ministry demands rootedness for endurance. The Christian life, especially for those who shepherd and oversee others, involves ongoing pressures and trials. Criticism comes. Discouragement sets in. Some seasons of life feel fruitless. Others, just dry. The temptation is to press forward in our own strength or to coast on past momentum. But that won't sustain the Christian pastor. Not for long. Only roots will.

But roots in what? Roots are not your ministry platform or personality. They're not being clever in sermon preparation or popularity in ministry circles. Roots aren't your influence on social media. Those things may grow branches, but they can't sustain the tree. Real endurance comes from what happens in secret—when no one is watching but God. That's where the strength and life are.

Rootedness is linked with daily dependence, done again and again. It means unhurried time in God's Word. It means prayer that's more than just saying words that sound good. It means communion with God that feeds the soul. It's linked with relationship. What matters is whether your roots are deep enough to hold when the storms come, the sun scorches, and the soil is dry. Jesus was clear: without roots, even joyful beginnings collapse.

At this point, we turn our attention to three ways to be rooted—personal devotion, prayer, and scripture reading. These are areas Scripture presents as essential for thriving and enduring.

Rooted In Personal Devotion

Personal devotion, in the Christian sense, is the deliberate and ongoing posture of the heart toward God. It is a life that seeks Him consistently and sincerely. It involves setting aside time to draw near to Him. It includes reading Scripture to hear God's voice, praying to commune with Him, and meditating on His truth. It's where the inner life is nourished and the soul is fed. Yet—as I needed to remind myself—the power is not in the disciplines themselves. These are means to a relationship with the God who made us and saved us. It's all about relationship with Him and pleasing Him.

In addition, personal devotion transcends motivation or desire. We're not referring to momentum from a pep talk or emotion from a motivational speech. Devotion is rooted in daily discipline—a steady, faithful rhythm of seeking God whether our hearts feel moved in the moment. Like the habit of eating or exercising, it should become an essential, regular part of who we are. Over time, devotion shapes the soul because it forms deep patterns and habits of faithfulness. This kind of spiritual discipline trains the heart to return to God repeatedly, and it's in this quiet consistency that long-term endurance is forged.

Personal devotion is how the heart stays soft in dry seasons and anchored in storms. It is where the Christian, especially the pastor, is reminded of what is true—about God, about the world, and about himself. Personal devotion is about staying alive. Psalm 119 captures this well:

> I rise before dawn and cry for help;
> I wait for your words (v. 147).

> Your testimonies are my delight;
> They are my counselors (v. 24).

David cried out early in the morning, and he meditated on God's Word at night. He confessed, pleaded, rejoiced, and waited. That's devotion. A life turned toward God again and again. Daniel is another example. Long before the lion's den, he had built a rhythm of prayer—three times a day, facing Jerusalem, offering thanks and supplication.

Joshua received a major leadership assignment when Moses died. He was told to lead God's people into the land. What was the one thing God emphasized in preparing him for that task? Devotion to the Word: "This Book of the Law shall not depart from your mouth, but you shall meditate on it day and night…. Then you will make your way prosperous, and then you will have good success" (Josh 1:8).

Pastors who meditate on the Word become anchored. They think theologically. They endure.

Ezra is another example. We're told that "Ezra had set his heart to study the Law of the Lord and to do it, and to teach his statutes and rules in Israel" (Ezra 7:10). The order is instructive: study first, then personal obedience, and then public ministry. This is a helpful pattern for all Christians and pastors.

The church in Smyrna was told, "Do not fear what you are about to suffer…. Be faithful unto death, and I will give you the crown of life" (Rev 2:10). That kind of faithfulness isn't born in a crisis. It's cultivated long before—in a life already steeped in prayer. The heart that regularly bows before God in private is the heart that stands firm when the pressure hits.

Personal devotion is where love is kept alive. A man, or church, can teach Scripture and still lose intimacy with Christ. This is seen in Jesus' messages to the seven churches in Revelation 2–3. Ephesus, for example, had doctrinal precision and moral integrity, but they had drifted in heart. Jesus' warning is sobering: "You have left your first love" (Rev 2:4 NKJV). Jesus noted they were doing good things, but their love for Him had waned, which had to be remedied. Devotion to truth without love for the Lord becomes cold and mechanical.

That's what personal devotion produces. A life that endures and a heart that stays alive. It's something that keeps one from losing the love and zeal for Jesus.

Rooted in Scripture

A pastor must feed on the Word of God to endure. Without the steady nourishment of Scripture, the mind dulls and ministry becomes mechanical. Sermons may still come. Responsibilities may still be met. But the soul goes dry. And in time, so does the fruit. Jesus said, "Man shall not live by bread alone, but on every word that comes from the mouth of God" (Matt 4:4). If that's true for every believer, it's all the more true for those who shepherd others.

While reading Scripture to discern correct doctrine, I also had to learn that Scripture speaks to my personal relationship with Jesus. For example, Jesus' words in John 15:4–5 about abiding in Him aren't just material for theological discussion. They're not merely a platform for debating topics such as eternal security. They're a personal call to examine whether I am truly abiding in Him—walking with Him, trusting Him. That passage wasn't just for others. It was for me. Likewise, Jesus' Sermon on the Mount has many doctrinal implications. But Jesus is also giving instructions for His followers that He expects from them. That includes me. I had to learn that Scripture involves not only doctrine, but also spiritual expectations.

Pastoral work involves counseling, discipling, teaching, leading, and listening. But as he does these, the pastor must listen to God. And that happens through Scripture. The Bible renews the mind (Rom 12:2), guards from sin (Ps 119:11), and fuels godliness (1 Tim 4:6). When regular intake is neglected, the source of life that undergirds everything else is quietly severed.

The psalmist prays, "Open my eyes, that I may behold wondrous things out of your law" (Ps 119:18). Isaiah says, "The Lord God … awakens Me morning by morning … to listen as a disciple"

(Isa 50:4 NASB). That quiet posture is what sustains when ministry feels heavy or fruitless.

Timothy had been grounded in Scripture since childhood. He had Paul as a mentor. Yet Paul told him to continue in the sacred writings (2 Tim 3:14–15). Why? Because "All Scripture is breathed out by God … that the man of God may be complete, equipped for every good work" (vv. 16–17). Timothy needed to remain in the Scriptures he was already familiar with. We can become familiar with the Word of God while losing our passion for it. Paul warns about this.

A pastor who is not rooted in Scripture will not endure. Without regular intake for personal nourishment, the soul dries out. And when trials come, there's no reserve of strength. Ministry may continue for a time by momentum, but eventually, the shallowness shows.

The pastor must be the first to hear the Word. We are disciples, before we are expositors. When we drift from the Word, even subtly, it catches up with us. Scripture must pierce us before it ever reaches the pulpit.

When the Word is feasted upon daily, it nourishes and sustains. It steadies. It doesn't guarantee life and ministry will be easy, but it produces endurance. Jesus commended the church in Philadelphia, not for their size or influence, but because they kept His Word (Rev 3:8). That's what He noticed. That's what He honored.

Ezra is a model here: "For Ezra had set his heart to study the Law of the Lord, and to do it and to teach" (Ezra 7:10). That's the pattern: intake, obedience, then teaching. When that order is reversed—when output exceeds input—the soul suffers, and so does the ministry.

The pastor who continues in Scripture is the one who lasts. When the Word lives in us, it bears fruit in season. When the roots run deep, the soul stays anchored. Pastors who stay rooted in Scripture will endure because they draw from a source that never runs dry.

Rooted in Prayer

Prayer is essential for rootedness. A pastor who doesn't pray won't endure. Wisdom is replaced by self-direction and self-reliance. And the soul drifts further from the One who supplies strength. The outward motions of ministry might continue for a while, but the inward life begins to wither. And eventually, the cracks show.

Prayer is the lifeline of the soul, the opportunity for us to speak directly and personally to our Maker. It is how we live in dependence. It is where the private battles are fought. It is where the heart is unburdened, and the will is surrendered.

Jesus modeled this. After a full day of ministry, when the crowds were pressing in, He rose "very early in the morning, while it was still dark" to go to a secluded place to pray (Mark 1:35). His mission was weighty, and He knew what it was to draw near to the Father before engaging the world. If Jesus sought the Father in private, what does that mean for us?

Daniel was a man of unshakable conviction in the midst of a hostile culture. But the roots of his strength were in prayer. Three times a day, he knelt and gave thanks to God, even when a death sentence involving the lion's den hung over him (Dan 6:10). It was his habit before danger came. And that habit made him stable in crisis.

In Acts 6, the apostles, faced with real ministry needs, refused to be drawn away from the foundation. They said, "But we will devote ourselves to prayer and to the ministry of the word" (Acts 6:4). The pressures were real, and the people needed leadership. Widows were being overlooked in the serving of food, and that needed to be addressed. But they knew they couldn't lead well without prayer and the Word of God.

Psalm 62:8 urges, "Trust in him at all times, O people; pour out your heart before him; God is a refuge for us." Prayer is pouring out your heart before God. Paul echoes this in Philippians 4:6–7: "do not be anxious about anything, but in everything by prayer and supplication with thanksgiving let your requests be made known to God." And what follows? "The peace of God … will guard your hearts and your minds in Christ Jesus."

Pastors need that peace. They need that refuge. And it is found in prayer. A place where endurance is cultivated and where strength is renewed.

Isaiah 40:31 states, "but they who wait for the Lord shall renew their strength; they shall mount up with wings like eagles; they shall run and not be weary; they shall walk and not faint." Waiting on the Lord isn't passive. It's the pattern of a servant who knows that he can't lead unless he first seeks God.

Conclusion

I've seen this with myself and others over the years. The moments I've felt most weary and dry were not due to external circumstances. They can be traced back to a neglected inner life. Sometimes I let the cares of the world and of ministry carry me away from my relationship with God. It was subtle and never intentional. Cutting corners here and there. A week with hurried devotions, or sometimes no devotions at all. Prayer became mechanical or nonexistent. Then weeks became months. And then dryness and lack of vitality occurred.

That's why enduring with roots matters so much. Staying rooted is about relationship with God. It's the difference between coasting or getting by and truly overcoming and persevering. And it's about finishing well.

Ministry can be demanding. But pastors who make personal devotion, scripture reading, and prayer a refuge find the strength needed to persevere.

2

FACING THE WINDS: STANDING STRONG THROUGH ADVERSITY

Jimmy Carter

Known for their twisting limbs and their draping of Spanish moss, the southern live oak is perhaps the most iconic tree of the southern United States. Mature trees can reach a height of eighty feet, and the knotty limbs extend as far as one hundred eighty feet.7 People and animals are often found on hot summer days resting in the shade of these southern staples, classic symbols of antebellum estates and southern charm.

Those who study the live oak marvel not only their stunning appearance but also their remarkable resilience. The strong wood was used by the United States Navy to construct its first six frigates, and the living trees are renowned for their ability to stand firm in the face of extreme winds. [8] Again and again, hurricane ravaged areas find

---

7   Sophia Abolfathi, "Florida's Champion Live Oak Tree Stands Tall – A New Statewide Record-Holder in Alachua," *WUFT | News and Public Media for North Central Florida*, 4 October 2023, http://www.wuft.org/human-interest/2023-10-04/floridas-champion-live-oak-tree-stands-tall-a-new-statewide-record-holder-in-alachua.

8   "USS Constitution - Boston National Historical Park (U.S. National Park Service)," n.d., http://www.nps.gov/bost/learn/historyculture/ussconst.htm.

their live oaks face the storms with remarkable resilience. [9] How can a tree withstand such an assault? The answer concerns their expansive root system, which is one-and-a-half to two times the width of the visible tree. The winds rage, the branches bend, but the roots hold firm.

Those who dedicate their lives to the proclamation of the Word of God herald a glorious gospel to a lost and dying world. Though they come with the best good news the world has ever heard, they must be prepared to withstand inevitable winds of adversity. Like a tree planted on the coast, fierce winds are unavoidable for those who minster the Word of God. From betrayal by trusted partners to mocking and public slander, ministers should expect to suffer. How can the servant of the Lord stand firm when the storms of ministry come? He must have deep roots, firmly planted and ready to support when the winds howl. God's Word provides three such roots for sustained ministry in 2 Timothy 4:1–8.

As he wrote his final epistle, the apostle Paul was imprisoned in Rome. He knew his death was imminent and knew that false teachers were causing trouble in churches such as Ephesus where Timothy was serving. As the apostle put pen to paper one final time, he wrote to encourage and exhort Timothy to press on in the face of adversity. He called him to stand against fierce winds by living a life rooted in mission, doctrine, and perspective. Like a live oak firmly rooted in the sands, the life of a minister in Paul's day and today must remain rooted if it is to withstand the winds of ministry.

Rooted in Mission

2 Timothy 4:1–8 contains perhaps the most personal and powerful section in the entire letter. In the first three chapters, Paul lays a

---

9   "New Orleans' Urban Forest Survived Katrina," n.d., http://www.nbcnews.com/id/wbna9773202.

foundation, warns Timothy of false teachers, exhorts him to remain faithful, and reminds him of the unshakable authority of God's Word. As he transitions to the text before us, Paul finally articulates what has lingered just beneath the surface of his final epistle. He is about to die. These verses are the measured reflections of a man who knows his end is soon approaching. In the face of such knowledge, Paul's gaze is not turned inward in self-pity or fear. Rather, he sees the end of his life as an opportunity to reflect on the race he has run with the Lord and to encourage others to imitate his steps. He shares these reflections not to boast in himself, but to instill in Timothy and ultimately to every follower of Christ, a vision for enduring faithfulness. Despite doctrinal division and ministry challenges, Paul calls Timothy to stand firmly planted to the end. Timothy must remain rooted in his mission:

> I charge you in the presence of God and of Christ Jesus, who is to judge the living and the dead, and by his appearing and his kingdom: preach the word; be ready in season and out of season; reprove, rebuke, and exhort, with complete patience and teaching (2 Tim 4:1–2).

The apostle has come to the climatic section of his final letter to his beloved son in the faith (2 Tim 4:2). As he prepares for this last exhortation, Paul pulls out every stop. His command carries a profound weight as he invokes not only his own authority as an apostle but also the very presence of God the Father and Christ Jesus. With the audience set and Timothy paying close attention, Paul delivers five imperatives, commands issued "with the crisp forcefulness of a military order."[10] These are not suggestions or options; they are non-negotiable elements of faithful ministry that clarify Timothy's mission.

---

10   Thomas D. Lea and Hayne P. Griffin, *1, 2 Timothy, Titus* (vol. 34; The New American Commentary; Nashville: Broadman & Holman, 1992), 242.

First, Paul writes that Timothy is to "preach the word." This is the central command to which the next four imperatives relate.[11] The word carries the sense of a herald making a public announcement on behalf of a king.[12] Accordingly, it is the responsibility of the preacher to proclaim God's message, not his own thoughts. This proclamation may happen in a pulpit, but it also takes place in living rooms, coffee shops, and across kitchen tables. Whether in formal or informal settings, the mission must be in view. The faithful minister doesn't deliver homilies on society nor lofty speech or human wisdom (1 Cor 2:1–2). Instead, his mouth delivers the divinely inspired message of the King. His ministry is deeply rooted in the mission to exposit the Word of God.

Next, Paul calls Timothy to "be ready in season and out of season." He may be saying, "preach the Word when you feel like it and when you don't." More likely, his focus is on the attitude of the audience. He likely intended Timothy to understand something more like, "Preach when the people listen gladly, and when they want nothing to do with your message." This understanding better matches the context of verses 3–5. However this is translated, Mounce reminds that "the distinction is probably overly subtle; Timothy is to be about his task regardless of the situation."[13] Faithful preaching must not be governed by the hearers' preferences or responsiveness, but by an ongoing desire to fulfill the command to proclaim God's truth.

Paul ends these brief verses with three additional commands related to the manner of this preaching. He instructs Timothy to "reprove, rebuke, and exhort." To reprove is to confront error and

---

11   Robert W. Yarbrough, *The Letters to Timothy and Titus*, Pillar New Testament Commentary (Grand Rapids: Eerdmans, 2018), 435.

12   William Arndt, Frederick W. Danker, Walter Bauer, and F. Wilbur Gingrich, *A Greek-English Lexicon of the New Testament and Other Early Christian Literature*, 3rd ed. BDAG. (Chicago: University of Chicago Press, 2000), 384, s.v. "ἐπισωρεύω."

13   William D. Mounce, *Pastoral Epistles*, Word Biblical Commentary 46 (Dallas: Word, 2000), 573.

bring conviction. It's the corrective dimension of preaching that identifies falsehood and points to truth. If reproof is resisted, the preacher must then rebuke, which carries the idea of expressing a strong disapproval of someone or something.[14] Rebuke, however, isn't the final command given by Paul. For those who repent and for the faithful who need encouragement, the preacher is called to exhort. Ministry that's rooted in the mission of proclamation offers comfort, consolation, and a loving call to continue in the faith. This threefold approach requires not only courage but also a certain attitude.

While the flesh may be tempted to respond to adversity with anger, bitterness, or retreat, Paul insists that these commands must be done "with complete patience and teaching." As Mounce summarizes, "Timothy must have complete and total patience, and his teaching must inform his preaching, confronting, rebuking, and exhorting."[15] Patience is essential because spiritual growth is slow. Patience is necessary because people are prone to wander.

As ministers face the inevitable winds of ministry, they must first remain rooted in their mission. They are called to proclaim the Word of God. Paul's vision is not for an impulsive preacher but for a steady shepherd who lovingly and wisely teaches the truth over time, with long-suffering devotion. Paul's call is for faithful ministers who herald the Word of God.

Rooted in Doctrine

Some time ago I came across a disturbing disease wreaking havoc on the sheep flocks of England. Sheep scab, which results in a nearly insatiable itch, affects approximately nine percent of flocks annually and causes an estimated economic loss of 80–200 million pounds

---

14   BDAG, s.v. "ἐπιτιμάω," 384.

15   Mounce, *Pastoral Epistles*, 573.

each year.[16] Infected sheep first begin to rub against objects seeking relief. When that fails, they begin to bite at their fleece in a desperate desire to satiate the itch. Eventually if not addressed, the sheep begin to lose their wool and develop scabs all over their skin. If the disease persists, the unquenchable itch leads to weight loss, decreased appetite, and even death.

What itchy flocks fail to understand is they can't be cured by their own efforts. Their ailment is caused by microscopic mites which are treatable only by medicine. These tiny creatures are nearly invisible to the naked eye, and impervious to the desperate biting and scratching of sheep. Only a veterinarian or a good shepherd equipped with the correct medicine can provide a lasting remedy.

As we consider Paul's second key to ministry success, we transition from the call to ministry rooted in mission and focus on the need for a ministry rooted in doctrine. Paul describes not an itchy sheep, but itchy ears belonging of people looking for relief in all the wrong places.

> For the time is coming when people will not endure sound teaching, but having itching ears they will accumulate for themselves teachers to suit their own passions, and will turn away from listening to the truth and wander off into myths. But as for you, always be sober-minded, endure suffering, do the work of an evangelist, fulfill your ministry (2 Tim 4:3–5).

Why did Paul place such emphasis on the need for faithful proclamation of the Word of God in verses 1–2? He gives his answer here. Paul warns of a coming time, a time already seen in his day, when people "will not endure sound teaching." People will no longer put up with

---

16   Emily Joanne Nixon, Ellen Brooks-Pollock, and Richard Wall, "Sheep Scab Spatial Distribution: The Roles of Transmission Pathways," *Parasit. Vectors* 14 (2021): 344, https://www.doi.org/10.1186/s13071-021-04850-y.

or accept the healthy doctrine found in the Word of God. Though they're desperate for a solution to life's issues, they won't bear the truth Timothy had just been commanded to preach. Instead, they'll turn away from sound doctrine and accumulate teachers who tell them what they want to hear.

Rather than turn to the inspired words of life (John 6:68), those with itchy ears make themselves the standard for acceptable teaching and seek those who meet their standard. Instead of submitting to God's authoritative Word, they chase myths, seeking validation rather than transformation. As Paul describes their actions, he pictures men and women piling up an abundance of teachers who will give them what they believe they need.[17] In the end, this effort can never address the true issue. That requires a faithful shepherd equipped with the proper spiritual medicine.

As others turn from truth, Timothy and every subsequent minister must remain steadfastly rooted in doctrine. As men and women seek false teachers who will tickle their ears, and as winds of opposition increase against those who remain rooted in God's Word, those who minister should take great encouragement from Paul's challenge to Timothy. He exhorts his young son in the faith to "be sober in all things, endure hardship, do the work of an evangelist, fulfill your ministry." Timothy must think clearly, suffer patiently, proclaim the gospel boldly, and complete the task assigned to him by the Lord regardless of the opposition he faces. The contrast could not be clearer. While others provide ear-tickling messages sought by the masses, the man of God must proclaim the soul-piercing message given by the King. He must remain firmly rooted in accurate doctrine.

---

17 Frederick Lange, "σωρεύω, ἐπισωρεύω," in *Theological Dictionary of the New Testament: Abridged in One Volume TDNTa*, ed. Gerhard Kittel and Gerhard Friedrich, trans. Geoffrey W. Bromiley (Grand Rapids: Eerdmans, 1985), 1150.

Rooted in Perspective

In the closing verses of this section Paul turns at last to his own life. He offers himself as an example of a life well spent for the gospel. In 2 Tim 4:6–8, Paul borrows an illustration from the Old Testament sacrificial system. Numbers 28:4–7 records that the daily offerings in the tabernacle included a lamb, a grain offering, and a drink offering. This drink offering was typically oil or wine poured out to complete the sacrifice. A sacrifice was not just an animal dying, it was often pictured as a meal being offered to God. With this vivid imagery in mind, Paul writes,

> For I am already being poured out as a drink offering, and
> the time of my departure has come (2 Tim 4:6).

Paul sees his entire life as a living sacrifice. This is, after all, the same man who wrote to the church in Rome, "I appeal to you therefore, brothers, by the mercies of God, to present your bodies as a living sacrifice, holy and acceptable to God, which is your spiritual worship" (Rom 12:1). As Yarbrough observes, "Paul has lived out this mandate over the years, which has landed him where he now sits as he writes or dictates: death row."[18] Paul didn't think of himself as a martyr or one going to execution. Instead, he was offering the last drops of his life as a completion of the sacrifice to God.

Paul again states it plainly in 2 Timothy 4:6b, "the time of my departure has come." The Greek word translated "departure" is rich with imagery. Wiersbe summarizes that this word can mean to hoist anchor and set sail, signaling release from this world and entry into eternity.[19] It can also mean to strike a tent, suggesting the end of a

---

18   Yarbrough, *The Letters to Timothy and Titus*, 443.

19   Warren W. Wiersbe, *The Bible Exposition Commentary* 2 (Wheaton, IL: Victor Books, 1996), 255.

temporary dwelling.[20] Finally, it can refer to the release of a prisoner.[21] From Paul's current perspective, death is not loss but instead an opportunity to be released from his earthly body (2 Cor 5:1–8), a chance to set sail into eternity, and ultimately his freedom.

From his present perspective, Paul shifts his attention to his life leading up to that moment. He writes in verse 7, "I have fought the good fight, I have finished the race, I have kept the faith." Paul envisions his life as a boxer who battled to the end, a runner who never strayed from the course, and a steward who never squandered the treasure of the gospel. His aim was never comfort or popularity, but faithfulness to his Lord. As he reflects on his walk with Christ, he's reminded of what truly mattered.[22] His walk with the Lord had been like that of Moses who prayed "teach us to number our days" (Ps 90:12).

Looking beyond the present and the past, Paul turns his gaze to the future. Verse 8 concludes, "Henceforth there is laid up for me the crown of righteousness, which the Lord, the righteous judge, will award to me on that day." Athletes in Paul's day sacrificed for years to receive a wreath of woven branches. Paul was also motivated by the promise of a future reward, but he had something far better in mind. He anticipated an eternal crown of righteousness by Christ, an award available "not only to me but also to all who have loved his appearing" (2 Tim 4:8b). Paul's past, present, and future were firmly rooted in an eternal perspective. He endured to the end with an anxious anticipation of his home going to heaven.

Conclusion

As we reflect on Paul's words to Timothy, we are confronted with challenges and encouragement. As the winds of ministry howl, God's

---

20 Wiersbe, *The Bible Exposition Commentary*, 255.

21 Wiersbe, *The Bible Exposition Commentary*, 255.

22 Wiersbe, *The Bible Exposition Commentary*, 255.

Word calls all who minister on His behalf to stand against the gusts, firmly rooted and standing till the end. Faithful servants should live in such a way that their mouths proclaim God's Word, their ears remain tuned to His truth, and their lives are lived daily as a living sacrifice.

Like the beautiful southern oaks, those in ministry must live lives firmly rooted and prepared for the storms that will come. They must remember the mission and preach the Word in favorable and unfavorable seasons. They must remain rooted in doctrine and teach biblical truth rather than ear-tickling messages. And finally, they must maintain a proper perspective, offering themselves daily as a living sacrifice as they anticipate the day they will enter the presence of the King. As the winds of ministry blow, may those who minister in the Lord's name rely on His strength, remain firmly rooted, and strive to finish well their course assigned by their King.

3

PRUNING FOR GROWTH: HANDLING CRITICISM AND CONFLICT

Les Lofquist

In every season of ministry, a pastor will encounter criticism. It's unavoidable. No matter how faithfully we serve, there will be seasons when words will wound, and conflicts will arise. Criticism often feels like a personal attack, a rejection not only of what we have done, but of who we are.

Yet Scripture forces us to see criticism differently. In God's sovereign hand, even the sharpest criticisms can become instruments of grace. Jesus taught His disciples, "every branch that does bear fruit he prunes, that it may bear more fruit" (John 15:2). Pruning is painful, but pruning is purposeful. Without it, growth would stall, and fruitfulness would be stunted.

Criticism and conflict, properly understood and handled, can be two of God's primary means of pruning His shepherds for greater effectiveness. Learning to deal with them wisely is essential for every pastor who desires long-term, faithful ministry.

Understanding the Nature of Criticism

Criticism comes in many forms, from many sources, and with many motivations. Understanding the nature of criticism helps us respond with wisdom rather than woundedness.

One of the most vivid biblical examples of criticism comes in the life of David (2 Sam 16:5–14, 30). David, who was already devastated by the tragic betrayal of his son Absalom, encountered Shimei hurling rocks and violently cursing him. The scene is painful, raw, and deeply emotional.

From this powerful narrative, we observe some of the ugly aspects of severe criticism and by application, we can consider when and how criticism arrives in our lives as pastors today. Note the following about criticism in David's life:

- Criticism came when he least needed it: David was vulnerable and overwhelmed—exhausted emotionally, physically, and spiritually. He was in no condition to defend himself or process this level of hostility with any kind of understanding. Often, criticism strikes us when we are already staggering under heavy burdens, making it feel even more devastating.

- Criticism came from someone outside the central conflict: Shimei was not directly involved in Absalom's rebellion but seized the moment to vent his own long-standing bitterness. Similarly, critics today may inject themselves into crises they barely understand, using another's pain as an opportunity to air their own unrelated grievances.

- Criticism came from someone least qualified: Shimei's own life and reputation were questionable. He was not a respected counselor nor a godly voice. In ministry, it is common for criticism to come from those lacking spiritual maturity, theological depth, or firsthand knowledge of the situation.

- Criticism came in the least helpful form: instead of offering constructive feedback or genuine concern, Shimei hurled accusations, curses, and rocks. The form of criticism matters. Destructive criticism—full of anger, half-truths, and/ or mockery—rarely seeks resolution and instead inflicts unnecessary wounds.

- Criticism came from someone whose intent was simply to harm: Shimei's goal was not David's restoration but David's humiliation. He wanted to hurt David. He just wanted to throw rocks. Some critics, fueled by resentment or jealousy, simply want to tear down rather than build up. Their aim is not the good of the pastor or the mission but their own satisfaction in seeing the pastor suffer.

Pastor, understand that the painful timing and hurtful nature of criticism do not negate the potential usefulness under God's sovereign hand. David's story reminds us that the timing and tone of criticism, however unjust, do not rob it of its ability to be used by God for refinement. Even hostile words, when placed under the wise hand of the Lord, can sharpen our character, humble our hearts, and drive us deeper into His grace.

Criticism Sometimes Masks Deeper Issues

Not every critic says what he means. In Numbers 12:1–2, Miriam and Aaron criticize Moses over his Cushite wife, but the real issue was jealousy over Moses' leadership. Similarly, Paul faced superficial criticism of his appearance and speaking style (2 Cor 10:10), while underlying tensions about his apostolic authority simmered beneath.

Critics sometimes focus on surface issues to avoid acknowledging other deeper struggles of pride, fear, or control. Wise pastors learn to listen beyond the words to discern the true spiritual dynamics at play.

Criticism Can Be Projection

Another subtle reality is that some criticism is more about the critic than the criticized. In 2 Samuel 12:5–6, David, guilty of his own hidden sin, reacts harshly to a parable about injustice which was actually a projection of his own guilt into the allegory Nathan presented.

Critics sometimes project their unresolved sin, insecurity, or painful past onto others, such as their pastor. Recognizing this possibility allows a pastor to respond to the critic with compassion and discernment, avoiding unnecessary defensiveness.

Criticism May Be an Attack of the Enemy

Criticism is not always purely human in origin. Nehemiah 6:5–9 shows how opposition to God's work often involves calculated criticism, which is designed by our unseen enemy to intimidate and derail the work of God.

Pastors must remember that our true struggle is not "against flesh and blood" (Eph 6:12). Some criticism, especially when aimed at stifling gospel ministry, must be recognized as spiritual warfare. In such cases, godly resistance, prayer, and perseverance are our weapons.

Criticism Often Arises from Incomplete Information

Many criticisms stem not from malice, but from misunderstanding. Decisions made with prayerful wisdom can be misconstrued when all the facts are not presented by the church leaders or known to the critics. Miscommunication by the pastor and elders can inflame otherwise faithful hearts in the congregation.

In these moments, patience, clarity, and humility exhibited by the pastor can diffuse tension. A soft answer, a careful explanation, and a sincere openness can go far to restore trust and defuse the critics.

Criticism Is Sometimes Entirely Unjustified

David's long suffering under Saul's jealous rage provides a sobering reminder that some criticism is wholly unjust and sinfully given. Despite David's loyalty and integrity, Saul pursued him mercilessly for years.

At such times, it is vital to keep a clear conscience before God, resisting the urge to defend oneself vindictively. David entrusted his reputation to God, trusting that "The Lord rewards every man for his righteousness and his faithfulness" (1 Sam 26:23).

Sometimes Criticism Is True

Perhaps this is the hardest reality of all—sometimes our critics are right. David, even during Shimei's unjust cursing, humbly acknowledged the possibility that God had allowed it for his correction (2 Sam 16:10–12). David's willingness to consider that there might be truth in even a hostile rebuke reflects a heart tender before God.

Another biblical example comes from the leadership of Joshua. After the miraculous victories at Jericho and Ai, Joshua and the elders made a grave mistake by entering a covenant with the Gibeonites without seeking the counsel of the Lord (Josh 9:18). When the people of Israel later discovered the deception, they grumbled against their leaders and criticized them. Though the complaint arose from the people's frustration, it was based on a legitimate failure in leadership: Joshua and the leaders had acted presumptuously, trusting appearances rather than pursuing God's guidance. In this case, the criticism pointed to a real lapse in spiritual discernment.

Both David's and Joshua's examples remind us that leaders are not infallible. A wise pastor doesn't automatically reject criticism, even when it stings or seems poorly timed. Instead, he asks prayerfully, "Is there truth here that I need to take to heart?" Growth often lies on the far side of painful honesty.

Honest reflection under the light of God's Word can transform painful correction into profound spiritual growth. Humility in receiving justified criticism not only protects our own hearts but also models for the flock what it means to walk in repentance and dependence on God.

A Framework for Handling Criticism

Given the complex and often emotional nature of criticism, how should pastors process it in a way that honors God, promotes personal growth, and serves the church faithfully? Handling criticism well requires deliberate reflection and spiritual discernment. The following framework offers a biblically rooted approach for pastors facing both fair and unfair criticism.

Consider the Source

Who is offering the criticism? The character and spiritual maturity of the critic matters significantly. Proverbs 27:6 reminds us, "Faithful are the wounds of a friend; profuse are the kisses of an enemy." Criticism from a spiritually mature believer who loves the Lord, loves you, and understands Scripture deserves special attention, even when it's painful. On the other hand, a harsh word from someone walking in bitterness, rebellion, or immaturity should be weighed more cautiously. While all criticism can be an opportunity for growth, not all critics are equally credible. As pastors, we must ask—is this coming from someone who is wise, knows me, loves Christ, and seeks the good of the church?

Moreover, it must be remembered that sometimes God uses unlikely sources—even enemies—to bring needed correction (2 Sam 16:10–12). Thus, considering the source requires both wise discernment and humble openness.

Consider the Spirit of the Criticism

Equally important is the spirit in which the criticism is offered. Is it presented in a spirit of prayerful love, humility, and a desire for restoration, or is it delivered in anger, pride, or resentment? Proverbs 15:1 teaches, "A soft answer turns away wrath, but a harsh word stirs up anger." A critic's tone, posture, and manner often speak louder than the words themselves.

A word spoken in love can pierce the heart in a way that leads to repentance and growth, while a word spoken in anger may provoke defensiveness and division. Wise pastors learn to listen carefully not only to the content of a critique but also to the heart behind it, discerning whether the critic seeks to build up or to tear down.

Consider the Number of Critics

A single complaint may reflect a personal preference, a misunderstanding, or an isolated offense. However, when multiple individuals raise similar concerns independently, it may indicate a deeper issue requiring attention. Scripture affirms the importance of multiple witnesses when evaluating a matter (2 Cor 13:1, Deut 19:15).

Patterns are often more significant than isolated incidents. Wise leaders will pay close attention to recurring themes or repeated feedback. If several trusted voices identify the same weakness in you or concern about you, humility calls for careful self-examination and possible corrective action. As the Yiddish proverb states—if one man calls you a donkey, pay him no mind; if two men call you a donkey, get a saddle. Ignoring repeated counsel can harden the heart and eventually erode effective ministry.

Weigh Specific Criticism More Heavily Than Vague Criticism

Specific, actionable feedback is generally more trustworthy than vague expressions of dissatisfaction. Vague complaints such as "you're just not leading well" or "people are unhappy" or "I'm not being fed" provide no clear direction for correction or growth. However, when criticism identifies clear issues—such as inconsistent communication, a pattern of impatience, or lack of pastoral care in one particular instance—those specifics can be prayerfully addressed.

Pastors shouldn't necessarily be quick to discount general concerns, but they should prioritize specific criticisms that name behaviors, actions, or omissions that can be evaluated against Scripture and corrected with God's help. Proverbs 18:13 warns against responding to a matter before hearing it fully; alternatively, asking clarifying questions can turn vague feedback into specific, helpful insight.

Reflect Calmly and Prayerfully

Emotional reactions to criticism are natural but rarely helpful. James 1:19–20 exhorts, "every person be quick to hear, slow to speak, slow to anger; for the anger of man does not produce the righteousness of God." Reacting impulsively—whether with anger, defensiveness, or self-condemnation—clouds judgment and poisons relationships.

Instead, pastors must learn to pause, pray, and seek God's perspective. Silent reflection allows the Holy Spirit to work in the pastor's heart regarding both the truth and the error in a criticism. It also enables pastors to disentangle legitimate concerns from emotional noise. Calm, prayerful processing ensures that responses are shaped by wisdom and love, rather than wounded pride.

Taking time to reflect, praying through relevant Scriptures, and seeking solitude can often bring clarity that immediate and impulsive reactions will obscure.

Consult Trusted Counselors

Pastors shouldn't bear the weight of criticism alone. Inviting trusted, spiritually mature counselors into the process can provide invaluable perspective. Proverbs 11:14 reminds us, "Where there is no guidance, a people falls, but in an abundance of counselors there is safety." Wise counselors can help distinguish between healthy correction and unhealthy, even toxic, attack.

Sometimes, those closest to us—family members, fellow elders, or long-time ministry partners—can see blind spots we miss or can offer encouragement when unjust criticism strikes. Their input can prevent overreaction, clarify misunderstanding, and provide strength for a wise and gracious response.

Involving trusted counselors also cultivates accountability, reminding the pastor that he is not above correction but is called, like every believer, to grow in grace and truth.

Resolve the Issue

After reflection and consultation, pastors must act decisively. If a criticism is found to be valid, repentance and appropriate corrective action should follow swiftly. Such responsiveness models Christlike humility for the congregation and strengthens pastoral credibility. Proverbs 9:8–9 notes that wise individuals welcome correction and grow from it.

On the other hand, if after prayer and counsel the criticism proves unfounded, it must be consciously and prayerfully released. Carrying unresolved criticism—whether fair or unfair—can foster lingering bitterness, paralyzing self-doubt, and unnecessary spiritual burden.

Resolution, whether through repentance or release, frees the heart to continue serving with joy and clarity. As Paul exhorts in 2 Timothy 2:24–26, pastors are called to correct opponents with gentleness while remaining steadfast and faithful in the face of challenges.

A Model: Handling Criticism and Conflict in Acts 6

The early church offers an example of a wise response to criticism and conflict. This example came in a thriving congregation where tensions arose that threatened unity. Conflict arose when everything was going well and "and the disciples were increasing" (Acts 6:1a); spiritual momentum did not immunize the church against relational challenges.

Interestingly, the conflict was not over doctrine (6:1b). It concerned practical matters of daily ministry—specifically, the neglect of Hellenistic widows in the distribution of food. Many church conflicts today similarly arise from misunderstandings, overlooked needs, or feelings of inequity rather than from theological error.

The apostles listened carefully (6:2). They didn't dismiss or minimize the complaint, nor did they allow pride or defensiveness to cloud their judgment. Instead, they acknowledged the validity of the concern and moved quickly toward resolution.

They engaged the critics directly (6:3), inviting those raising the concern to be part of the solution by selecting qualified leaders. In doing so, they respected the congregation's voice while maintaining healthy oversight.

At the same time, the apostles stayed committed to their primary calling (6:2–4), refusing to be distracted from the ministry of the Word and prayer. They demonstrated that pastoral priorities must be guarded, even as administrative needs are wisely addressed.

The congregation responded positively (6:5). The apostles' wise and humble leadership fostered trust, and the solution brought greater unity rather than deeper division.

The final outcome was remarkable—the church grew even more (6:7). "The word of God continued to increase," and even a group of priests became obedient to the faith. Acts 6 reminds us that when criticism and conflict are handled well, they lead not to division but to growth. Conflict, when addressed with wisdom and humility, can become the catalyst for deeper health, a stronger congregation, and greater gospel advance.

Character Required: Pastors and 1 Timothy 3

Paul's description of pastoral character in 1 Timothy 3:3 highlights three crucial virtues that are especially vital for handling criticism with grace and maturity. First, a pastor must be "not pugnacious" (*mē plēktēn*), meaning he is not to be combative, quick-tempered, or given to violent reactions. An elder doesn't fight with his fists. A pugnacious spirit turns every disagreement into a battle, often damaging relationships and discrediting the gospel. In contrast, a true shepherd must have a calm and steady disposition, refusing to meet hostility with hostility.

Second, Paul calls pastors to be "forbearing" (*epieikēs*), a term that means to be gentle, reasonable, and considerate. Forbearance reflects a willingness to endure personal wrongs with patience, to listen thoughtfully, and to respond with kindness even when provoked. This spirit of gentleness mirrors the heart of Christ, who dealt tenderly with both the weak and the wayward.

Third, a pastor must be "uncontentious" (*amachos*), literally "not a fighter." Rather than escalating tensions, a faithful leader seeks peace, striving to defuse conflict rather than inflame it with his words. An elder doesn't fight with his mouth. He isn't easily drawn into endless arguments or petty disputes. Together, these virtues form a portrait of pastoral resilience—a man strong enough to endure criticism without retaliation, wise enough to respond with measured grace, and committed enough to prioritize unity over personal vindication. Such character is not optional for the pastor; it's essential for shepherding well in a fallen world where criticism is inevitable.

When others speak against you, resist the urge to defend yourself. Walk in humility, remembering that if they truly knew your heart, their words could be even harsher. Life's rebukes and challenges lose their sting when you've already faced your own faults honestly. Acknowledge the depths of your own need for God's grace. Anchor yourself in Christ, because genuine humility softens your heart before God and others. Pastors must model tender strength by receiving criticism with humility, responding with patience, and leading with courageous love.

Conclusion: Strengthening Yourself in the Lord

When criticism strikes, and it inevitably will, pastors must find their ultimate strength not in themselves, not in their reputation, but in God alone.

David understood this well. In 1 Samuel 30:6, we are told that when David was "greatly distressed," he strengthened himself in the Lord. His example wasn't one of denial or anger but of honest dependence. In the wilderness, during some of his darkest seasons, David penned songs of deep trust and longing, pouring out his heart with raw honesty before the Lord (Pss 57, 63). His cries were not signs of weakness but of a profound faith rooted in God's steadfast love.

The wisdom literature of Scripture also points us to a godly response. Proverbs advises, "The beginning of strife is like letting out water, so quit before the quarrel breaks out" (Prov 17:14). It commends the patience and humility required to overlook minor offenses (Prov 19:11), a posture that protects both heart and ministry from unnecessary wounds.

The New Testament echoes this call to gracious strength. Paul urged Timothy to correct opponents "with gentleness" (2 Tim 2:23–25), recognizing that the goal is not personal vindication, but spiritual restoration. Similarly, Paul charged the Corinthians, "Be watchful, stand firm in the faith, act like men, be strong. Let all that you do be done in love" (1 Cor 16:13–14). True pastoral strength is a combination of conviction and compassion, courage and kindness.

Criticism and conflict, painful though they are, offer pastors an unexpected gift—the opportunity for deeper reliance on Christ, fuller sanctification, and richer ministry fruit. They strip away self-reliance and drive us to our knees, reminding us that apart from Christ, we can do nothing (John 15:5).

Pastor, embrace the pruning. It's not a sign of God's displeasure, but of His preparation. Under His careful hand, you are being shaped for greater fruitfulness—for His glory, for the good of His church, and for the joy of your own soul. Trust the Vinedresser. In time, you will see that even the hardest cuts were made by the hand of love.

4

GUARDING AGAINST DROUGHT: AVOIDING BURNOUT

Peter Goeman

Introduction

The Texas A&M Forest Service reported the 2011 drought, the worst in Texas history, resulted in the death of 301 million trees.[23] Unlike sudden disasters, drought is a slow-moving killer that chokes life from the land over weeks, months, or even years. As such, drought becomes a useful analogy for the spiritual life. The psalmist appeals to this picture when he says, "For day and night Your hand was heavy upon me; My vitality was turned into the drought of summer" (Ps 32:4 NKJV).

Many resonate with these words. Feelings of despair and a lack of joy can be caused by various circumstances and situations that arise from living in a fallen world. One of the more common experiences that leads to feeling as though one's "vitality is turned into the drought of summer" is burnout. We can define burnout as being chronically overwhelmed and feeling physically, emotionally, mentally, and spiritually depleted.

---

23 "Texas A&M Forest Service Survey Shows 301 Million Trees Killed by Drought," *Texas A&M Forest Service* (blog), September 25, 2012, https://www.tfsweb.tamu.edu/texas-am-forest-service-survey-shows-301-million-trees-killed-by-drought.

Church leaders especially struggle with burnout. In a 2024 article, Religion News Service reported that fifty-three percent of American clergy had considered leaving the ministry due to burnout.[24] This feeling of exhaustion is not limited to church leaders. According to a 2014 article, Lifeway Research notes that seventy percent of mothers with children at home reported feeling overwhelmed by stress and not getting enough rest.[25]

How can Christians protect themselves from this trend? To help us minimize the possibility of burnout, I would like to direct our attention to three biblical principles that will help us become, for the sake of the analogy, a well-watered tree. These principles include being grounded steadfastly in the Word of God, relying entirely upon the Lord through prayer, and training our expectations to be realistic and in line with God's will.

Principle One: Be Grounded in God's Word

It would be laughable to expect a car to work without a power source, whether gasoline or battery. Even more ridiculous is the idea that a Christian could thrive in life without a continual grounding in Scripture.

The Bible consistently testifies to the importance of the Word of God in the life of a believer. One of the ways Scripture illustrates this is by portraying the Word's relationship with its hearers as water nourishing the land. For example, Isaiah pictures the Word of the Lord as rain or snow that comes down to water and refresh the land (Isa 55:10–11). Similarly, Psalm 1 portrays the man of God as a

---

24   Michael Woolf, "Burned Out, Exhausted, Leaving: A New Survey Finds Clergy Are Not OK," January 25, 2024, https://www.religionnews.com/2024/01/25/burned-out-exhausted-leaving-a-new-survey-finds-clergy-are-not-ok/.

25   Chris Adams, "5 Ways to Help Stressed Out Women in Your Church," October 30, 2014, https://www.lifewayresearch.com/2014/10/30/5-ways-to-help-stressed-out-women-in-your-church/.

well-watered tree, planted by the streams of water (Ps 1:3). The reason Psalm 1 describes this individual as a well-watered tree is because "his delight is in the law of the Lord, and on his law he meditates day and night" (Ps 1:2), linking the meditation on God's Word to the picture of being a steadfast, flourishing tree.

The Word of God is essential for the believer who desires to live a life of fulfillment, pleasing the Lord in every area. Here are three reasons being grounded in God's Word is a potent antidote to burnout.

God's Word Reveals His Will

Organizations or companies that lack a clear goal or purpose often die the death of impotency. It is a simple truth that people who don't know what they're trying to accomplish will lose focus and become discouraged. However, God has not left His people without guidance. His Word gives us insight and direction into our purpose and how we can discern God's will for our lives.

Psalm 119:105 says, "Your word is a lamp to my feet and a light to my path." It is God's Word that helps us see the path we must follow. This gives us a purpose. It should come as no surprise that the key to fulfillment for us as creatures is to obey what the Creator has mandated. Here are just a few of the things God has mandated:

1. The believer is to obey God's authoritative structure in creation (Rom 13:1).

2. The believer is to obey God's call to holiness (1 Pet 1:16, 1 Thess 4:3).

3. The believer is to obey God's call to love God and others (Matt 22:37–38).

4. The believer is to obey God's command to be filled with the Word (Col 3:16).

One reason Christians become discouraged and disheartened is that they're not following God's plan for their lives. Christians who are grounded in God's Word will have the confidence that they are doing what God wants them to do. Following God's will gives the believer a sense of purpose and confidence that begets endurance even amid difficulty.

God's Word Sanctifies

In one of the most emotional passages in all of Scripture, Jesus prays for His followers that God would "Sanctify them in the truth" (John 17:17). To remove any doubt as to what He is referring to, Jesus clarifies, "your word is truth." In this brief statement, the believer receives guidance on where to find the means of spiritual growth and sanctification. Sanctification occurs through the power of the Holy Spirit, mediated by God's Word.

It is sadly the case that church leaders (and Christians generally) often try to serve the Lord while besetting and unconfessed sins plague their lives. This is a recipe for disaster! I've known individuals who are laboring in ministry while struggling against the sins of lust, pride, anger, or envy. It is no wonder they feel exhausted and drained.

Being consistently in the Word helps feed our souls and provides the antidote to sin. God's Word shines like the light of the sun, its brilliant rays sweeping through the hidden corners of our hearts and banishing every lingering shadow. Therefore, we must be grounded in Scripture to foster the sanctifying work of the Lord in our lives.

God's Word Restores and Refreshes

One of the beautiful qualities of God's Word is that it revives the soul and rejoices the heart (Ps 19:7–8). I recall speaking with a young man who was deeply struggling with life and felt no joy. When I asked him about his daily Bible reading, he mentioned that he hadn't read the Bible in weeks. After gently admonishing him, I encouraged him to spend time daily in the Word. A week later, I asked him how things were going, and he said it was as if a fog had been lifted. He was encouraged to fight against sin, and his soul had been revived. It was the work of the Spirit of God through the Word of God.

Whenever we're feeling discouraged or down, even if there is no unconfessed sin in our lives, the solution must involve spending time in the life-giving Word of God. The Word is not simply a philosophical treatise on a variety of issues. The Word itself performs a supernatural work in our hearts, reviving them and bringing us joy. Neglecting regular time in the Word is like removing yourself from the very means God has given to nourish your soul.

Principle Two: Rely on the Lord through Vibrant Prayer

I have never met someone who thinks their prayer life is exactly what it should be. Churches are filled with conversations where someone asks, "How is your prayer life?" To which the response comes quite naturally, "It could be better." However, the sad reality is that for many Christians, a prayer life needs to exist before it can be improved.

The Bible teaches us that prayer is not an optional addition to the believer's life. It's a foundational part of what it means to be in relationship with God. Someone has said that prayer is to the Christian what breathing is to the human. Without prayer, there can be no spiritual life.

Prayer is the most direct way by which we relate to and connect with God. The command to pray is frequent throughout the New Testament. For just one example, in Philippians 4:6 Paul writes, "do not be anxious about anything, but in everything by prayer and supplication with thanksgiving let your requests be made known to God." When we live life this way—submitting our anxieties, worries, and difficulties to the Lord in prayer—we are promised, "the peace of God, which surpasses all understanding, will guard your hearts and your minds in Christ Jesus" (v. 7). There's a direct connection between our faithful and genuine prayers and the promised peace of God which will guard our hearts and minds.

Many times we struggle in doubt or exhaustion because we've not availed ourselves of the ever-present help that the Lord loves to provide. Sometimes we forget that the Lord wants us to cry out for help. As the psalmist says, "When the righteous cry for help, the LORD hears and delivers them out of all their troubles" (Ps 34:17). Indeed, the very next verse emphasizes, "The LORD is near to the brokenhearted and saves the crushed in spirit."

The point is simple. A life of constant prayer is not only commanded (cf. 1 Thess 5:17, Col 4:2) but also essential. We don't have the strength on our own to live as we ought, so we rely on the Spirit through prayer to give us strength. To deprive ourselves of a vibrant, intensive prayer life is to cut off the connection to the very giver of life itself.

Principle Three: Have the Right Expectations

Unmet expectations are often the cause of unhappiness or emotional exhaustion. In the words of Proverbs 13:12, "Hope deferred makes the heart sick, but a desire fulfilled is a tree of life." Thus, it's imperative to have the right expectations in the Christian life to avoid the emotional rollercoaster that can be a persistent temptation.

Paul's Ministry Advice (2 Tim 2:1–7)

> You then, my child, be strengthened by the grace that is in Christ Jesus, and what you have heard from me in the presence of many witnesses entrust to faithful men, who will be able to teach others also. Share in suffering as a good soldier of Christ Jesus. No soldier gets entangled in civilian pursuits, since his aim is to please the one who enlisted him. An athlete is not crowned unless he competes according to the rules. It is the hard-working farmer who ought to have the

> first share of the crops. Think over what I say, for the Lord
> will give you understanding in everything.

One of the most profound texts on the Christian mindset is 2 Timothy 2:1–7. In this text, Paul reminds Timothy that the Christian life can be illustrated by three pictures: the good soldier, the athlete, and the hard-working farmer.

The Christian ought to think of his life like the life of a soldier. A soldier doesn't get days off. He must be ready for battle every minute of every day. A soldier knows that a loss of focus will result in disaster for the whole army. Christians need to have a passion to serve their master in the same way the soldier is obligated to serve his commanding officer.

Additionally, the Christian life mirrors the athlete's journey, marked by discipline, endurance, and unwavering focus toward a defined goal. Athletes are marked by sacrifice. I was particularly impressed years ago when I read about the routine of twenty-three-time gold medal athlete Michael Phelps. When I read of his workout routine—three-a-day practices, extra dry-land workouts, regimented naps, and dietary restrictions—I was blown away. He had no life outside of swim training. He had denied himself many legitimate enjoyments in life that we often take for granted, but he did so for a greater goal of competing to the best of his ability. The Christian life is quite similar; we should be willing to deny ourselves and even suffer discomfort for an ultimate goal.

Similarly, the picture of the hard-working farmer is appropriate for the Christian. The farmer doesn't get vacations. He plants regardless of the circumstances, because if he doesn't plant, there will be no harvest. Farmers are tenacious examples of hard work, often making significant personal sacrifices for the sake of their work.

This threefold picture of the Christian life is powerful. When we come to Christ, we aren't signing up for a self-centered form of living. We come to die to self and live for Christ (cf. Luke 14:26–27).

Keeping in mind the pictures of the soldier, the athlete, and the farmer will help us keep the right mindset as we face trials in this life.

Wrong Expectations Will Lead to Unfulfillment

Expectations often color a situation either negatively or positively. How many of us have gone somewhere expecting to have a terrible time, and when our expectations were exceeded, we enjoyed ourselves? On the other hand, unmet expectations are the cause of conflict and dissatisfaction (cf. Jas 4:1–3). For example, if I give you a thousand dollars, you will probably be happy enough. I mean, who wouldn't appreciate such a gift? However, if I promise you a million and then fail to deliver, giving you *only* a thousand, you'll be disappointed and, most likely, angry. Interestingly, the context of a situation and the expectations involved often determine the emotional outcome. One's expectations or perception will influence the emotions positively or negatively.

The same principle applies in the spiritual realm as well. My wife and I have the privilege of doing a fair bit of premarital counseling. One of the things we often stress to soon-to-be-wed couples is that expectations can be quite dangerous in marriage. A wife can quickly find herself upset with her husband because he violates her preconceived expectation of what their time on Friday night would look like, and the husband can become frustrated with the wife because she doesn't think like a guy. Having the wrong expectations in marriage can lead to conflict, sometimes significant conflict.

In a similar sense, if we hold incorrect expectations in the Christian life, we will be unhappy and unfulfilled. If we expect God to give us something, or we expect people to treat us a certain way, we will regularly face disappointment and emotional distress. Having the wrong expectations is a sure-fire way to face burnout in the Christian life.

In an interview, John MacArthur was asked a question about discouragement and its relationship to ministry. This was his answer:

So, you know, don't be under any illusion, men, that this is a bed of roses, and you—I tell you what; people talk about burnout all the time, "Well, you know, burnout, burnout, burnout." Nobody ever got burnout from hard work. Plumbers don't get burnout. Ditch diggers don't get burnout. This kind of burnout, this kind of discouragement usually is connected to unrealistic expectations … of yourself, for yourself, for your ministry that aren't met. And that's what winds you down into depression. So, what I tell people is expect nothing. You don't deserve anything so expect nothing.[26]

This is good advice for Christian ministry, but it is also good advice for the Christian life. We ought to strive to model the attitude that Jesus told us to embody—"We are unworthy servants; we have only done what was our duty" (Luke 17:10). Whatever the Lord wants to do with us, may He do so for His glory. Ironically, when we lower our expectations and take the mindset of the slave, serving for the glory of God, it is that much more difficult to burn out.

Practical Advice for Avoiding Burnout

Having examined three biblical principles that will help provide a proper foundation, it would be helpful now to offer some practical advice for avoiding burnout. Obviously, the above principles are the core strategy for combating burnout. But as image bearers of God, we are both physical and spiritual beings. As such, our physical habits impact our perception of life. Thus, even non-Christians in the medical field have observed that physical habits improve one's mental

---

26 "A Personal Glimpse: Al Sanders Interviews John MacArthur," *Grace to You*, March 8, 2001, https://www.gty.org/sermons/GTY76/a-personal-glimpse-al-sanders-interviews-john-macarthur.

stamina and state.[27] It is with this in mind that I offer seven practical pieces of wisdom.

Get Physical Exercise

We are told explicitly that "bodily exercise profits a little" (1 Tim 4:8, NKJV), but unfortunately, many Christians live as though "bodily exercise profits not at all." Yet, physical exercise has many benefits—both in the long term and the short term. Regular exercise helps alleviate stress and enhances your body's overall efficiency. God created us to do physical hard work, and those of us who sit for long periods of time especially need to engage in regular exercise.

Get Enough Sleep

Although some Christians think they are capable of surviving on less sleep (especially with the power of coffee), the majority of Christians need more sleep than they usually get. Sometimes that's just the season of life that we are in, but we should prioritize sleep as a way to serve the Lord. Sleep is an underutilized tool in preparing us for faithful ministry.

Eat Healthy

We live in a time where eating habits are emphasized, so I don't need to comment much on it. I will simply say that it's now beyond doubt that our diet affects our emotions and energy. If athletes and

---

27   Christopher James Holland, Michale Cole, and Jennifer Owens, "Exercise and Mental Health: A Vital Connection," *British Journal of Sports Medicine* 58, no. 13 (July 1, 2024): 691, https://www.doi.org/10.1136/bjsports-2024-108562. According to the authors, "Regular physical activity significantly reduces symptoms of depression, anxiety and stress while enhancing cognitive function and self-esteem. Even a single bout of exercise can reduce anxiety, and short-term engagement can buffer against stress-induced negative mood states."

academics recognize the importance of maintaining a healthy diet for physical and mental well-being, shouldn't Christians also view this as an essential part of stewardship?

Avoid Screen Time

Although screens are a relatively new challenge, we can already see that excessive screen time is having adverse effects on society.[28] One is that prolonged screen time from TV, phone, iPad, computer, etc., results in a feeling of lethargy and exhaustion. These feelings of emotional exhaustion can be dealt with easily by putting the phone away and going for a walk.

Rest without Being Lazy

Rest is an important part of our lives. We need it, and we need it regularly. However, we live in a society where we can rationalize the pursuit of pleasure under the heading "rest." But we ought to train ourselves to find rest in things that truly refresh us. You may think you are resting by watching an all-night Lord of the Rings marathon, but that will not bring rest. R. C. Chapman was well known for his Saturday resting ritual of woodworking. We need to be intentional about how we rest and train ourselves to rest in productive ways.

Avoid Overcommitment

One of the most common culprits of exhaustion is overbusyness— often resulting from the inability to say no. Church leaders especially are tempted to get involved with everything, but the wise Christian

---

28 Brett McCracken and Ivan Mesa, eds., *Scrolling Ourselves to Death: Reclaiming Life in a Digital Age* (Wheaton, IL: Crossway, 2025).

understands that we have limitations. Our main focus should be on clear, God-given priorities.

Train Yourself in Thanksgiving

This may seem like an odd practical step to avoid burnout, but it's important. When we train ourselves to be thankful (and we can!), we're filled with joy and wonder at what God is doing in our lives. It's difficult to become discouraged or burned out when you're constantly reminded of the blessings God has graciously given to us. The psalms are filled with the call to remember the blessings of God (cf. Ps 77:11; 103:2; 105:5; 143:5, etc.). When we meditate on God's goodness, maintaining the proper perspective on life becomes easier.

An Important Clarification

At this point, I need to make a necessary clarification. It is *not* inherently sinful to feel overwhelmed or physically exhausted. We all go through difficult days or even seasons of life where we struggle, and that is not evidence of a sinful life. It is, of course, possible that unconfessed sin is the cause of feeling overwhelmed or physically exhausted. Solomon noted that "envy makes the bones rot" (Prov 14:30b), and David said before he confessed his sin, "my bones wasted away through my groaning all day long" (Ps 32:3).

However, even if we are unaware of unconfessed sin, we need to prudently evaluate our lives to see whether we're being unwise in how we're living. Even then, if we endeavor to live a life of wisdom (which includes adequate rest), it may be that the Lord has allowed us to experience emotional challenges as part of the normal struggle of humanity living in a fallen world. There should be no guilt over this, but Christians should soldier on, casting their troubles upon the Savior (1 Pet 5:7) through a life of prayer (both their own and the prayers of others).

Conclusion

In the same way that a tree can't thrive in parched soil, the Christian cannot endure life's difficulties without being rooted in the living water of God's provision. By anchoring ourselves in Scripture and by coming before the throne in ceaseless prayer, we rely on God's strength, not our own. When we also embrace realistic expectations—seeing ourselves as soldiers on watch, athletes in training, and hard-working farmers—we guard our hearts against the temptations and distractions of unfulfilled longings and desires. The principles in this chapter won't keep us from difficulty, but, Lord willing, they will help us endure the trials of life. God, in His grace, will sustain us through obedience to the commands of Scripture and by applying wisdom to our daily lives.

5

NURTURING THE BRANCHES: BALANCING FAMILY AND MINISTRY

Doug Bookman

The business of balancing ministry duties and family responsibilities is one of the most difficult and delicate challenges faced by every right-hearted believer, but the issue is certainly the more acute for those in vocational ministry. Helpful counsel is to be had from many noble quarters, but I would suggest that there is stunningly rich example, instruction, and encouragement to be found in the life of Jesus.

An important note: the remembrance of the earliest Christian community is that Joseph, Jesus' adopted father, died sometime after Jesus' experience at the temple at the age of twelve (Luke 2:42–50—the last time Joseph appears in the narrative) and before Jesus went to be baptized at the age of thirty (Luke 3:23). More importantly, the Gospel record bears compelling inferential witness to that reality: during the three years of His public ministry Jesus encounters His family several times, and Joseph is never mentioned. If Joseph were still alive, he certainly would've played a role in those encounters. And finally, Jesus' giving Mary to the care of John the apostle demonstrates clearly that her husband had died.

For purpose of this study, the biographical reality to be emphasized and contemplated in that regard is this: when His adopted
father died, Jesus, as the eldest son, would have assumed leadership
over that family. And as we'll see, the biblical record is clear that He
did. Thus it is legitimate and encouraging to ponder the reality that
Jesus knows what it is to watch over a family, and thus to balance
those two sacred and occasionally competing responsibilities. We will
ponder that reality as we focus on five times when Jesus encounters
His own family in the Gospel records.

A Moment of Tender
Leave-Taking (John 2:1–10)

Five days after Jesus emerged from the ordeal of fasting, temptation,
and angel-assisted recuperation in the Jeshimon wilderness of Judea
(Matt 4:1–11, Mark 1:12–13, Luke 4:1–13), Jesus arrived at a family wedding in the city of Cana (cf. John 1:29, 35, 43; 2:1 to trace
the five days). This is the first time Mary has seen her son since several weeks earlier when He set out from Nazareth to be baptized by
John the Baptizer, and it is obvious that some dramatic changes had
occurred. We know from the other Gospels that an important change
had occurred as Jesus rose from the waters of the Jordan River—the
Spirit had descended on Jesus and pressed Him into the Messianic
ministry that He desired since the age of twelve (Matt 3:16–17, Luke
2:49). But Mary didn't know that had happened!

And yet Mary had known from the moment an angel confronted
her as a betrothed virgin (Luke 1:26–33) that this supernaturally con-
ceived child was in fact the long-awaited Messiah-Deliverer of Israel
(cf. Mary's song, Luke 1:46–55). But for three remarkable decades
He had lived a stunningly normal, delightfully pleasant life as her
baby, her toddler, her youngster, her eldest bar-mitzvahed son—and
then for some years as the leader and primary provider of her family.
What must she have thought when now, after an unexpected absence
of several weeks, He shows up at a family wedding accompanied by

the "calling card" of a rabbi in that culture—disciples! And now a crisis: to a degree hard to appreciate today, to "run out of wine" at a wedding is an unthinkable social *faux pas*.

Mary knew well from the Scriptures that the Messiah would be a worker of miracles, and that in the kingdom of the Messiah "they shall sit every man under his vine and under his fig tree" (Micah 4:4, Zech 3:10)—that is, that the fruit of the vine would flow in abundance. And so she makes of her son a reasonable, motherly entreaty—"They have no wine" (2:3). And thus, this tender scene of leave-taking as Jesus says to His mother, "Woman, what does your concern have to do with Me? My hour has not yet come" (John 2:4).

Jesus' words sound harsh, but they are not. He addresses His mother as "Woman," and that is as deliberately impersonal as it sounds. Importantly, He refrains from calling her "Mother," because the precious close and constant "mother-eldest son" relationship that they had known for three decades was now to be changed.[29]

Jesus is not abandoning His mother or His family, but he is "fine-tuning" the dynamics of that relationship. This is precisely what He meant by the next statement, "what does this have to do with me?" (ESV, literally: "What to me and to you? [τί ἐμοὶ καὶ σοί]). That statement is a Hebraism, an idiom used several times throughout the Bible (cf. Judg 11:12; 1 Kgs 17:18; 2 Chr 35:21; Matt 8:29). It always conveys a sense of distancing or a clarifying of the dynamics of a relationship. It is not rude or hostile; it is meant to draw the listener to consider the relationship between him and the speaker.

And finally, Jesus responds directly to Mary's request: "My hour has not yet come!" This is often taken as a cryptic reference to the hour of His death, but Mary couldn't have understood it to mean that. Jesus' reference is to the miracle she has requested. He is gently

---

29 The only other time Jesus refers to Mary as "Woman" is from the cross as He turns her over to John for spiritual safe-keeping (John 19:26–27)—another moment of leave-taking.

but firmly insisting that He can no longer simply respond to His mother's needs and desires as He had done so happily and carefully for all these years. Now He must wait on the timing and direction of the Holy Spirit. And Mary, having long anticipated this moment, understands that; she simply steps aside and directs the servants to do as Jesus commands.

For purposes of our study, note the defining sense of *priorities* articulated by Jesus in this scene, the animating awareness that His primary focus and allegiance must be to the ministry on which He has now embarked. But note as well the gentleness and patience with which He impresses this upon this one whom He loved so dearly. Jesus knows what it is to tenderly but firmly maintain proper priorities in the effort to balance family and ministry.

From Nazareth to Capernaum
(John 2:12, Matt 4:13)

Very early in His public ministry, for identifiable strategic reasons, Jesus relocated from Nazareth to Capernaum. From that point in the narrative Capernaum is "his own city" (Matt 9:1), and He is "at home" there (Mark 2:1). The immediate strategic genius of the move is apparent—Nazareth sat on a bluff overlooking the Jezreel Valley. It was hard to reach and on the way to nowhere. Capernaum, on the other hand, was the center of taxation for Galilee. Herod Antipas administered that jurisdiction, and he insisted that all the roads leading there be carefully maintained. Thus, Jesus moved to Capernaum in anticipation of an intense itinerant preaching ministry which would have Him traveling repeatedly to every corner of that region.

Another reason isn't so obvious, but perhaps more important with reference to the spread of the gospel. Throughout the Bible ages, Israel was the most important chokepoint on the most important international trade routes in the world. Every day, scores of caravans moving goods and travelers across the world would pass through

Galilee, and every one of them would be routed into Capernaum to pay the required tolls and fees.

At the same time, the Gospels are explicit that people from other lands were bringing their sick to Jesus to be healed (Matt 4:24, 25; Mark 3:7–10). Because Jesus was frequently gone on "preaching tours" throughout the region, folks would very often go to the city where Jesus lived with His family to wait for His return. So when Jesus did return there would be great crowds awaiting Him, so much so that made it difficult for Him to get into the city to eat (Mark 3:20). Each return would allow another remarkable season of healing (Matt 4:24, 8:16). Indeed, the proportion of Jesus' miracles specifically recorded as happening in Capernaum is remarkable.

Here is the connection. Because of the caravan traffic, on any given day there were hundreds of travelers in Capernaum on their way to every corner of the world but idle for a little while as they waited for the "wagon master" to attend to the taxes. They would surely have hastened to witness the scene as the sick were brought to the Nazarene, and He "laid his hands on every one of them and healed them" (Luke 4:40). But shortly every one of those stunned travelers would rejoin his caravan as it made its way to this or that corner of the world. And then in days to come, as the good news was taken to "all the world," when an apostle or evangelist arrived in that traveler's town and read from the Gospel of Matthew the accounts of the miracle-working Nazarene, and as our traveler's townspeople wagged their heads and insisted, "Such a thing cannot be!" that traveler could bear eyewitness testimony—"No! I was in that land! I saw blind children given sight, lame men throw away their crutches, women with every sort of infirmity healed in a moment! The Nazarene was a miracle worker, and so the claim that He returned from the dead is not so unbelievable as you think!" Thus was the entire world "salt-and-peppered" with eyewitness testifiers to the reality of the stories of a wonder-working Jew named Jesus of Nazareth.

So, for reasons strategic to His ministry and the spread of the gospel, Jesus moved His home from Nazareth to Capernaum. But for purposes of our study the point to be made is that *He took His family with Him* (John 2:14). In that culture, you remained in the village where you were born, and so did you children and their children after them. All of life—your synagogue, your clan, your workmates, your relationships—were built around your neighborhood. The most compelling evidence that Jesus had assumed the leadership of His family is that when, for reasons basic to His ministry, He relocated to Capernaum, He brought His family with Him.

Though we have no record of tension and resentment on the part of Jesus' siblings over this disruption of their lives, we can reasonably assume there was some. But Jesus weathered it. This provides inferential but instructive testimony to the fact that Jesus knows what it is to struggle with the difficult balance between ministry and family, specifically to shepherd His family through the difficult seasons of life which arose because of His commitment to ministry.

Jesus' Broken Heart (Mark 3:20–35)

Well into His eighteen-month ministry in Galilee, evidently as Jesus returned with His apostles to His home in Capernaum after a grueling "preaching tour," He was greeted by a such a multitude "that they could not even eat" (Mark 3:20). In response, "his mother and his brothers" (i.e., His family, cf. v. 31) "went out to seize him, for they were saying, 'He is out of His mind'" (v. 21). The unfolding scene is one of gut-wrenching emotional angst and disappointment for Jesus:

> And his mother and his brothers came, and standing outside they sent to him and called him. And a crowd was sitting around him, and they said to him, "Your mother and your brothers are outside seeking you." And he answered them, "Who are my mother and my brothers?" And looking about at those who sat around him, he said, "Here are my mother and my brothers! For whoever does the will of God, he is my brother and sister and mother (Mark 3:31–35).

Work hard to imagine that moment! Do you suppose that Jesus loved His family any less than you or I love our families? That He spoke these words with a dry cheek?

Interestingly, Jesus is here living up to an important Old Testament ethic. Because Levi and Simeon had done wickedness to the people of Shechem (Gen 34), Jacob had declared that they would not receive a portion in the promised land (Gen 49:5–7). But later at Mount Sinai it was Levi who answered the call to put to death all who were involved in the wickedness of the golden calf incident (Exod 32:26–28). And then, as Moses blessed the twelve tribes, Jacob's curse on Levi was amended. That tribe would not have their own portion, but they would be made the priestly family—they would live in priestly towns and eat from the tithes of the people. And this explicitly because of the choice Levi made at Mt Sinai when that tribe "said of his father and mother, 'I regard them not;' he disowned his brothers and ignored his children. For they observed your word and kept your covenant" (Deut 33:9).

And so it was with Jesus on that unspeakably awful day when His brothers came to take Him, thinking he was mad! When the decision was before Him as to whether He would give His allegiance to His earthly family or His heavenly Father, He made the choice that was morally right but bottomlessly hurtful. God forbid that we— whether in the context of vocational ministry or otherwise—should be faced with that decision. But if so, what an encouragement to know that our Savior can be "touched with the feeling" of that very heartache (Heb 4:15 KJV).

Jesus Is Mocked by His Unbelieving Brothers (John 7:1–9)

The account here is simple. It is autumn, and the Feast of Tabernacles is at hand. Jesus will die in the coming spring at the Feast of Passover. No one knows Jesus of Nazareth better than His half-brothers. No one has seen the truth so constantly, compellingly and compassionately taught and lived out as they had in their decades of life with Jesus. Certainly no one had been prayed for and witnessed to more carefully than they had been by their elder brother. And yet, "His brothers did not believe in Him" (John 7:5 NKJV). As they set out for the feast they scoffed at Him and His claims (7:3, 4). But in the face of that derision, Jesus responds honestly, firmly, and gently:

> Then Jesus said to them, "My time has not yet come, but your time is always ready. The world cannot hate you, but it hates Me because I testify of it that its works are evil. You go up to this feast. I am not yet going up to this feast, for My time has not yet fully come." When He had said these things to them, He remained in Galilee (John 7:6–9 NKJV).

The ensuing story of Jesus' travel to the Feast in Jerusalem "as it were in secret" (7:10) is intriguing and instructive. But for the purpose of our study, the focus is on Jesus' persevering concern for His brothers. To be sure, the claims made by Jesus to His brothers—the claim to be not only the long-awaited Messiah but also to be God come in the flesh (John 20:30–31)—were difficult to accept. But His brothers had seen thousands of the sign-miracles which demonstrated that Jesus was indeed speaking for the God of Israel (John 2:2). And they knew—more intimately than most—that He was the fulfillment of scores of prophecies recorded in their Scriptures. Their unbelief wasn't born of a paucity of convincing evidence. And yet at this late point in His ministry, "His brothers did not believe in Him."

We will focus shortly on the happy turn this element of Jesus' biography takes. But the point to be made in our study is this—throughout all the months of His ministry, Jesus' heart was heavy with the awareness that those He loved most in this life had rejected Him and His claims. Jesus knows the frustration of family members who reject the truth in spite of the passion and compassion that truth is set before them by those who love them best.

Jesus' Love for Mary on the Cross (John 19:25–27)

Consider the indescribably poignant and tender scene. Jesus hangs on a Roman cross, engulfed in a vortex of incomprehensible physical and emotional anguish, anticipating the infinitely more awful terror He will experience being "forsaken" by God—that is, when the infinitely blessed personal relationship He'd enjoyed with His heavenly Father from eternity is in some inscrutable and horrible way suspended, as He is judicially disfellowshipped by His Father. But now, in the hours before sunlight turns gray, He looks down and sees His mother standing by the cross. The defining detail to be inferred is that He does *not* see His brothers. Well might He have expected them to be there at least to support their mother. But they are not there. And thus, knowing that those who give their allegiance to Him will suffer greatly in the days to come (Luke 23:31) and being concerned for His mother's spiritual safe-keeping, Jesus assigns to John the apostle the responsibility to care for her.

For purposes of this study, ponder this. As Jesus suffered on that instrument of hideous torture and execution, His soul is made even heavier by this stark reminder of His brothers' stubborn disbelief. His heart surely rejoiced and angels danced in heaven when the dying thief next to Him repented, but one suspects that even then Jesus' delight must have been dampened by His remembrance of His brothers' impenitence. We all have hearts made heavy over loved ones who refuse to believe. It's certainly an encouragement to realize Jesus knows that heaviness in the most real sense.

But a final point to consider is this—we know the rest of the story. After His victory over death, Jesus appeared at least to the eldest of His brothers (1 Cor 15:7), and all of His brothers became believers and then leaders in the early Christian community (Acts 21:17). And thus a final note of hope for those of us for whom the struggle to balance ministry and family—and most importantly the effort to see our family bow the knee to the truth—turns distressing. The life that

Jesus lived before those siblings, His careful and compelling explanation of the truth concerning Himself, His repeated compassionate entreaties even in the face of intransigent and derisive disbelief—all of this was used by the Holy Spirit to bring Jesus' beloved siblings to repentance and faith. There's no guarantee here for us, but there's a precious and sustaining encouragement to faithfulness in our effort to balance family and ministry.

In sum, the sublimely encouraging affirmation of Scripture is that Jesus was "in *every respect* tempted as we are, yet without sin" (Heb 4:14). Included in that exhaustive phrase "in every respect" is the perpetual challenge and occasional heartache of balancing family and ministry. The record of the Gospels is clear—Jesus knew that specific trial of life. As Spurgeon meditated on Hebrews 4:14, "Ye tempted ones, come to your tempted Saviour, for He can be touched with a feeling of your infirmities, and will succour every tried and tempted one."[30]

---

30   Charles Haddon Spurgeon, *The Cheque Book of the Bank of Faith: Being Precious Promises Arranged for Daily Use* (New York: American Tract Society, 1893).

6

ROOTS INTERTWINED: THE STRENGTH OF COMMUNITY, MENTORSHIP, AND ACCOUNTABILITY

Andrew Burggraff

It's amazing how God has intricately created trees and the dense community of trees known as forests. Trees in a forest are stronger together; they form interconnected networks, both above and below ground, sharing resources and supporting each other through storms. This interconnectedness enhances the overall resilience of the forest ecosystem.

Trees that grow close together can survive powerful storms by supporting each other. A study conducted a few years ago reveals this important fact:

> Kana Kamimura at Shinshu University in Japan and her colleagues were monitoring two different plots of Japanese cedar trees, one of which had been thinned to assess whether giving individual trees more room to grow made them more vulnerable to wind damage, when typhoon Trami unexpectedly hit in early September 2018.... Kamimura and her team measured the stress forces experienced by the trees before, during and after the typhoon, and surveyed the resulting damage.

The plot that hadn't been thinned kept all of its trees, while the sparser plot lost many. The researchers think that the tight spacing helped protect the trees in the plot that weren't thinned by dissipating the force from the wind through collisions between branches of neighboring trees. This stopped the force travelling into the sensitive stem and roots below, where it might help uproot trees. They also found that the trees that did fall in the thinned plot didn't fail instantly but over time, like a piece of metal that's repeatedly been bent back and forth before finally breaking.[31]

The careful observer can anticipate the applications from this scientific study. The trees that were tightly compacted supported each other and survived the typhoon. The trees that were isolated didn't break immediately, but, over time, they were worn down and finally snapped. Like trees, ministers must not serve in isolation; rather, they must develop support systems for community, mentorship, and accountability.

The call to ministry is a beautiful and weighty invitation into God's work. Ministers are entrusted with guiding souls, communicating truth, walking alongside the suffering, and serving as shepherds of Christ's flock. Yet far too many who accept this call find themselves overwhelmed, isolated, and silently struggling. Ministry, while sacred, can be lonely. The emotional, spiritual, and physical demands placed on a minister are often invisible to the people they serve. Sad to say, many ministers who serve in isolation eventually bend and ultimately break. Many ministers leave the ministry because of the emotional toll, the physical exhaustion, the spiritual pressure on themselves and their families, the burnout of constantly bearing the weight of one's calling, or from spiritual/moral catastrophe.

---

31   Alex Wilkins, "Trees that Grow Close Together Are Better at Withstanding Storms," *New Scientist*, https://www.newscientist.com/article/2312031-trees-that-grow-close-together-are-better-at-withstanding-storms/.

In a recent Lifeway Research study, Mark Dance summarized the following facts concerning pastors:

- 84% say they're on call 24 hours a day.

- 80% expect conflict in their church.

- 54% find the role of pastor frequently overwhelming.

- 53% are often concerned about their financial security.

- 48% often feel the demands of ministry are more than they can handle.

- 21% say their church has unrealistic expectations of them.[32]

Due to the pressures, many pastors are considering leaving the ministry. A study conducted by the Barna Group reveals something similar:

> As of March 2022, the percentage of pastors who have considered quitting full-time ministry within the past year sits at 42 percent. This is consistent with data from fall 2021 when Barna first reported on a sharp increase in pastoral burnout, and it confirms the growing number of pastors who are considering resignation—up 13 percentage points from 29 percent in January 2021…. Over half of pastors who have considered quitting full-time ministry (56%) say "the immense stress of the job" has factored into their thoughts on leaving. Beyond these general stressors, two in five pastors (43%) say "I feel lonely and isolated."[33]

---

32 Mark Dance, "Pastors Are Not Quitting in Droves," *Lifeway Research*, https://www.research.lifeway.com/2019/07/10/pastors-are-not-quitting-in-droves-2/.

33 The Barna Group, "Pastors Share Top Reasons They've Considered Quitting Ministry in the Past Year," https://www.barna.com/research/pastors-quitting-ministry/.

Could an effective support system help prevent ministers from leaving the ministry? Mark Dance, in the above mentioned study, argues that pastors are not quitters but encourages the following: "Every pastor needs a pastor in their life and ministry. Who can you be a Barnabas to? If you're a lay leader in your church, treat your pastors like friends or family members, because they're both. Provide a listening ear and a safe place for your pastors to share their dreams, as well as their nightmares."[34]

In this chapter, we'll explore why ministers urgently need three key supports—community, mentorship, and accountability. These are not secondary concerns. They are vital structures that protect, strengthen, and sustain a leader's calling. When these elements are in place, ministers are more likely to lead with integrity, endure hardships with joy, and continue in the ministry to which they have been called.

The Power of Community: Never Meant to Lead Alone

The very nature of the gospel is relational. God exists in eternal community—Father, Son, and Holy Spirit. We were created in His image, not to live in isolation, but in fellowship with Him and one another. The church, described in Scripture as the body of Christ, functions through connection. Every member plays a part, and every part needs the others (1 Cor 12:12–27). Craig Blomberg, in his commentary on this passage, states the following:

> Body parts are interdependent, not independent of each other. The New Testament recognizes no individual or "lone-ranger" Christians who are not attached to some local Christian fellowship. That is not to say it is impossible to be

---

34 Mark Dance, "Pastors Are Not Quitting in Droves."

saved and uninvolved, merely that it is unhealthy. In societies where individualism is valued above corporate responsibility, the importance of the metaphor of Christ's church as a body looms large. Paul's emphasis on all of us needing every other believer greatly relativizes any hierarchy of status, rank, or privilege that we might otherwise try to establish.[35]

Pastors are not exempt from this divine design. If anything, they should be the most deeply embedded in the life of the body. Yet, many pastors find themselves emotionally distanced from the very community they lead. They often face unspoken expectations to be invulnerable, always ready to give but rarely positioned to receive. This disconnection is not only dangerous, it is unbiblical.

Ecclesiastes 4:9–10 reminds us, "Two are better than one, because they have a good reward for their toil. For if they fall, one will lift up his fellow. But woe to him who is alone when he falls and has not another to lift him up!" The implication is clear—isolation leaves us vulnerable. As Donald Glenn concludes, "Solomon lamented the perils of isolation."[36] When pastors lead in isolation, they are more likely to burn out, make unwise decisions, or fall into discouragement. Without others walking alongside them, even the most faithful shepherd can lose direction.

Hebrews 10:24–25 calls believers to "let us consider how to stir up one another to love and good works, not neglecting to meet together, as is the habit of some, but encouraging one another." This is not a suggestion; it's a command, even for leaders. In Heinrich von Siebenthal's Greek grammar, he states that the verb "let us consider"

---

35   Craig Blomberg, *1 Corinthians*, The NIV Application Commentary (Grand Rapids: Zondervan, 1994), 252.

36   Donald R. Glenn, "Ecclesiastes," *The Bible Knowledge Commentary: An Exposition of the Scriptures* 1 (Wheaton, IL: Victor Books, 1985), 987.

is a hortatory subjunctive that expresses a directive, "we must."[37] In addition, David Allen highlights that the verb "let us consider" also "conveys the concept of careful consideration, thoughtful attention and deep concern."[38] Believers, including ministers, must be in relationships that stir them to love and good works. Ministers need safe spaces where they can be encouraged, challenged, and reminded of the goodness of God in the context of real relationship.

The early church offers a powerful example of this concept. Acts 2:42–47 paints a picture of a community deeply committed to fellowship, breaking bread, prayer, and shared life. Their strength didn't come from polished programs but from profound connection. When ministers build these kinds of relationships (with peers, with trusted friends, and within the broader body), they create an ecosystem of health and grace around their leadership.

Community doesn't only offer support in hard times; it also brings celebration, laughter, and shared joy. It reminds pastors that they are primarily children of God, not employees of the church. As spiritual family members, we mutually support each other in the work of the ministry.

The Gift of Mentorship: Leading through Legacy

No leader arrives fully formed. Even those with great natural gifting require guidance, sharpening, and example. The Bible provides numerous examples of mentoring relationships (Moses and Joshua, Elijah and Elisha, Naomi and Ruth, Barnabas and Paul, Paul and Timothy). Each of these pairings illustrates God's method for developing leaders—life-on-life influence over time.

---

37   Heinrich von Siebenthal, *Ancient Greek Grammar: For the Study of the New Testament* (New York: Peter Lang, 2019), 352–353.

38   David L. Allen, *Hebrews*, The New American Commentary (Nashville: Broadman &Holman, 2010), 517.

Paul's words to Timothy in 2 Timothy 2:2 provide a blueprint for mentoring: "and what you have heard from me in the presence of many witnesses entrust to faithful men, who will be able to teach others also." Here we see a multi-generational chain of discipleship and mentorship. William Barclay states, "The teacher is a link in the living chain which stretches unbroken from this present moment back to Jesus Christ. The glory of teaching is that it links the present with the earthly life of Jesus Christ."[39] The first stage in the spiritual "relay" was "these things" being handed from Paul to Timothy. Timothy's obligation was to "run the second lap" in which he was to entrust the things Paul taugh him to other faithful men.[40] "Entrusting" these foundational truths of the gospel was not simply tapping another believer on the shoulder and providing basic encouragement. Rather, it would require Timothy to teach and to model the faith before others who in turn would teach and model the faith before others.[41]

For pastors, mentorship is critical. Many enter ministry with theological knowledge but little practical wisdom. A mentor provides the voice of an experienced spiritual elder who has walked the road and can offer insight born of scars and victories alike. Mentors can show how to navigate a congregational moral failure, a financial crisis, or the slow ache of ministry fatigue.

Throughout my own ministry journey, mentors have consistently played a vital role in offering wisdom and guidance, especially during challenging ministry situations. Fresh out of seminary, I encountered the most difficult counseling case I have faced to this day. Despite having taken several counseling courses, the complexity, depth, and far-reaching impact of the situation went far beyond anything I had

---

39   William Barclay, *The Letters to Timothy, Titus, and Philemon* (Philadelphia: Westminster, 1957), 182.

40   John MacArthur, *2 Timothy*, MacArthur New Testament Commentary (Chicago: Moody Press), 41.

41   Philip H. Towner, *The Letters to Timothy and Titus* New International Commentary on the New Testament (Grand Rapids: Eerdmans, 2006), 491.

been trained for in the classroom. I reached out to one of my pastoral mentors, who had also been my counseling professor in seminary. After hearing the details, his immediate response was "In all my years of ministry, I've rarely come across a case this difficult." Over the next several months, we had many conversations in which he offered invaluable biblical insight and counsel that helped me navigate the situation with wisdom and care. Without his support, I would've felt overwhelmed and risked giving unhelpful or even harmful advice.

Proverbs 27:17 says, "Iron sharpens iron, and one man sharpens another." Sid Buzzell stresses, "when iron is rubbed against another piece of iron it shapes and sharpens it. Similarly, people can help each other improve by their discussions, criticisms, suggestions, and ideas."[42] Bruce Waltke further explains,

> The analogy infers that the friend persists and does not shy away from constructive criticism. This persistent friend, whose wounds are faithful (v. 6) ... performs an indispensable task. As a result of his having a "hard" friend—a true one—a man develops the capacity to succeed in his tasks as an effective tool, and in the end he will thank his friend for being hard as flint.[43]

This sharpening process is not always comfortable, but it is necessary. Mentors can speak truth in love, ask hard questions, and challenge a leader to grow in character, not just competency.

Exodus 18 offers a striking example of mentoring in action. Moses, overwhelmed by the burden of judging the people alone, receives a visit from his father-in-law, Jethro. Jethro watches Moses at work and then says plainly, "What you are doing is not good. You

42   Sid S. Buzzell, *Proverbs,* The Bible Knowledge Commentary: An Exposition of the Scriptures 1 (Wheaton, IL: Victor Books, 1985), 964.

43   Bruce K. Waltke, *The Book of Proverbs: Chapters 15–31,* New International Commentary on the Old Testament (Grand Rapids: Eerdmans, 2005), 384.

and the people with you will certainly wear yourselves out, for the thing is too heavy for you. You are not able to do it alone" (Exod 18:17–18). With wisdom and clarity, Jethro helps Moses delegate responsibility and establish a healthier structure for leadership. Every pastor needs a Jethro, someone who can see the blind spots, name the unsustainable patterns, and speak with fatherly wisdom.

In addition, mentorship also combats pride. It reminds pastors that they're not the final authority, not the first to walk this road, and not immune to the need for guidance. It reinforces the truth that humble leaders are the most powerful leaders, because they are open to learning, correction, and growth.

The Safety of Accountability: Guardrails for the Soul

Of the three areas that are being discussed in this chapter, accountability may be the most uncomfortable and the most crucial. In a position of authority, ministers face a unique set of temptations—pride, isolation, moral compromise, spiritual apathy, and emotional exhaustion. Without structures of accountability, even the most well-meaning leader can slowly drift into dangerous territory.

James 5:16 exhorts believers to "confess your sins to one another and pray for one another, that you may be healed. The prayer of a righteous person has great power as it is working." This is not simply about confession; it's about healing. J. Ronald Blue states the following regarding this verse: "a mutual concern for one another is the way to combat discouragement and downfall. The cure is in personal confession and prayerful concern. The healing (that you may be healed) is not bodily healing but healing of the soul."[44]

Craig Blomberg further clarifies this idea of spiritual healing:

---

44 J. Ronald Blue, *James*, The Bible Knowledge Commentary: An Exposition of the Scriptures 2 (Wheaton, IL: Victor Books, 1985), 835.

Here it seems to refer to restored spiritual well-being due to confession and forgiveness. We ought to have people close enough to us whom we allow to inquire into our spiritual state, whether formally as with a pastor or elder, or more informally as with an accountability group, partner, or mentor. James makes it clear that the Christian life should not be lived apart from community.[45]

Accountability provides a context for honesty, repentance, and restoration. It's not about surveillance or suspicion, but about safety and soul care. Accountability is an expression of love. It acknowledges our vulnerability to failure and emphasizes the importance of extending both grace and truth to restore and support one another.

Unfortunately, some pastors avoid accountability—fearing exposure, judgment, or disqualification. However, real accountability isn't simply reduced to exposing sin; it's about preventing it. It's proactive, not simply reactive. It requires building trusted relationships where vulnerability is embraced, not penalized. True accountability demands the humility to accept hard truths from those who care enough to speak up. Accountability requires tremendous courage. Being honest and vulnerable about our sins and ongoing temptations is not easy. Yet, this kind of transparency paves the way for profound freedom in our spiritual journey.

For accountability to be effective, it must be intentional. Ministers shouldn't rely on informal or vague relationships to serve this purpose. Instead, they should actively seek out trusted peers, elders, or mentors who have permission to ask difficult questions, speak into blind spots, and pray fervently over their souls.

---

45 Craig L. Blomberg and Mariam J. Kamell, *James*, Zondervan Exegetical Commentary on the New Testament 16 (Grand Rapids: Zondervan, 2008), 245.

Conclusion: Shepherding the Shepherd

Pastors are not just shepherds; they are also sheep. Ministers belong to the flock of God and are in constant need of grace, growth, and guidance. Their calling is not to perform perfectly, but to walk faithfully with others. The myth of the lone leader, the untouchable figure of authority, is not only harmful, but also counter to what is taught in Scripture. Healthy leadership is rooted in humility, formed through relationships, and sustained by support.

So, to the minister feeling isolated—connect with a supportive community. Surround yourself with friends and fellow ministers who value you for being you, not just for what you do. To the one feeling burned out—seek a mentor to renew your sense of purpose and calling. To the one hesitant to be vulnerable, honest, and accountable—share your journey with a fellow minister who will listen with kindness and honesty.

You were never meant to minister for God alone. Just as trees in a densely populated forest withstand storms by supporting one another through interconnected networks, ministers too need strong connections to thrive in the often-turbulent landscape of ministry. In the beginning of this chapter, the Japanese cedar tree study powerfully illustrates the dangers of isolation and the strength found in unity. Trees that stood together endured the storm, while those left alone eventually gave way to persistent strain. In the same way, ministers who seek community, mentorship, and accountability position themselves for endurance and resilience. Ministry is a sacred yet demanding calling, and no one was meant to carry it alone. For the sake of their own well-being and the health of the church, ministers must resist isolation and lean into the strength that comes from walking together in faith.

7

NOURISHING GROWTH: EXPANDING KNOWLEDGE FOR LASTING FRUITFULNESS

Thomas Pittman

Introduction

Pastors, like all believers, are vulnerable to seasons of spiritual drought. Congregations often look to their shepherds for nourishment, guidance, and strength, yet pastors themselves must remain deeply rooted in God's Word if they are to endure. Scripture paints a vivid picture of this reality: "He is like a tree planted by streams of water, that yields its fruit in its season, and its leaf does not wither" (Ps 1:3, ESV). The vitality of the tree does not come from its own strength but from the water that continually sustains it. In the same way, a pastor's endurance flows not from natural gifting or human effort but from a steady supply of God's truth that refreshes the heart and equips him for every good work.

In the present age of ministry, pressures abound on every side. Cultural instability, rising expectations, and emotional fatigue weigh heavily upon those who lead God's people. Many pastors find themselves pulled in countless directions—preaching, counseling, administration, discipleship, and family responsibilities—each demanding energy and focus. Without intentional nourishment, such demands leave the shepherd drained and vulnerable to discouragement or burnout. Enduring fruitfulness requires more than determination; it requires the deep well of God's Word continually filling and sustaining the soul. A ministry that flourishes only at the beginning but withers over time is not what Scripture envisions for those entrusted with shepherding Christ's flock.

For this reason, ongoing learning must be embraced as a vital part of pastoral life. A pastor who continues to grow in the knowledge of God remains supple and fruitful even as the years pass. By contrast, one who ceases to learn slowly loses clarity, strength, and resilience in ministry. Continual theological growth, far from being a distraction from pastoral work, is the very root system that gives it life. Study and reflection are the hidden streams that produce visible fruit in faithful preaching, wise counsel, and steadfast leadership. By drinking deeply from the well of God's Word, pastors find both strength for themselves and nourishment for the flock.

This chapter explores the biblical and theological foundation for such growth. It will show that endurance in ministry is inseparably tied to theological depth and that spiritual maturity cannot be separated from a continual pursuit of learning. Drawing upon biblical exegesis, historical testimony, and the insights of faithful shepherds past and present, we will see that nourishing growth is essential for long-term fruitfulness. The pastor who plants himself firmly by the streams of God's truth will not only endure the challenges of ministry but flourish in a way that blesses the church and glorifies Christ. Such growth is not optional for the shepherd of God's people; it is the very means by which he fulfills his calling.

The Tree Planted by Streams: A Scriptural Foundation

Throughout Scripture, trees are presented as enduring images of stability, nourishment, and fruitfulness. From the very beginning, the tree of life stood in the garden of Eden as a testimony to God's sustaining power (Gen 2:9), and in the final vision of Revelation the tree of life reappears, yielding fruit for the healing of the nations (Rev 22:2). Proverbs describes wisdom as "a tree of life to those who lay hold of her; those who hold her fast are called blessed" (Prov 3:18, ESV), reminding us that wisdom is not merely theoretical but life-giving, nourishing those who seek it. In each case, the tree stands as a symbol of rootedness and growth that cannot be explained apart from God's gracious provision. For pastors, these images remind us that spiritual vitality is sustained only when the roots of ministry sink deeply into the soil of God's Word.

Psalm 1 provides perhaps the clearest expression of this truth. The psalmist compares the blessed man to "a tree planted by streams of water that yields its fruit in its season, and its leaf does not wither. In all that he does, he prospers" (Ps 1:3, ESV). Such a tree flourishes not because of its own power but because it continually draws life from the water beside it. This picture of ongoing nourishment offers hope to pastors who may feel weary in the midst of their labors. Fruitfulness in ministry does not ultimately depend on a leader's creativity, charisma, or stamina, but on his closeness to the Word of God. Even when the seasons change, the pastor who remains rooted by the stream will continue to bear fruit in due time, because his supply never runs dry.

Jeremiah echoes this same imagery in his prophetic encouragement: "He is like a tree planted by water, that sends out its roots by the stream, and does not fear when heat comes, for its leaves remain green, and is not anxious in the year of drought, for it does not cease to bear fruit" (Jer 17:8, ESV). Here the emphasis falls on endurance. The tree is not spared from heat or drought, but it remains fruitful because its roots reach deeply into a dependable source. Pastors also face seasons of difficulty, whether through cultural pressures, congregational struggles, or personal trials. Yet if their roots extend into the nourishing waters of God's Word, they need not be paralyzed by fear or overcome by discouragement. Just as the tree remains green in times of drought, the faithful pastor can remain fruitful in adversity because the source of his strength is unchanging.

This rootedness, however, does not occur automatically. It requires a deliberate choice to stay near the stream. For pastors, this means committing themselves to the ongoing study and meditation of God's Word. Paul charged Timothy to "do your best to present yourself to God as one approved, a worker who has no need to be ashamed, rightly handling the word of truth" (2 Tim 2:15, ESV), a command that assumes continual diligence in learning. Likewise, Peter exhorted elders to "shepherd the flock of God that is among you, exercising oversight, not under compulsion, but willingly, as God would have you" (1 Pet 5:2, ESV), which is impossible apart from being fed themselves. A shepherd cannot guide the flock to green pastures if he has not first eaten from them. The faithful pastor must drink deeply from the Word so that he is equipped to nourish others.

The writer of Hebrews warns against spiritual stagnation, lamenting that "though by this time you ought to be teachers, you need someone to teach you again the basic principles of the oracles of God. You need milk, not solid food" (Heb 5:12, ESV). He presses his audience to pursue maturity, declaring that "solid food is for the mature, for those who have their powers of discernment trained by constant practice to distinguish good from evil" (Heb 5:14, ESV). This is not merely a call for first-century believers but a continual reminder for pastors today. Ministry that is fueled only by what was learned in seminary or early in one's calling soon runs thin. Ongoing study guards against complacency and equips pastors with discernment to recognize both truth and error. A ministry that is rooted in God's Word remains alive, relevant, and fruitful even as challenges arise.

Theological Growth as a Guard against Drift

A faithful shepherd cannot afford to minister from a shallow well. Sound doctrine provides the ballast that steadies the ship of pastoral ministry and keeps it from drifting into error. Paul warns the church in Ephesians 4:13–14 that maturity in the faith and knowledge of Christ is what enables believers to avoid being "tossed to and fro by the waves and carried about by every wind of doctrine, by human cunning, by craftiness in deceitful schemes" (ESV). If this warning is true for every Christian, it is even more pressing for pastors who are called to guard both themselves and their flock. Theological growth is not an optional supplement to ministry but the very means by which endurance is cultivated and faithfulness is preserved.

Doctrinal drift often begins quietly and without fanfare. Sometimes it comes through neglect of serious study, allowing habits of reflection to grow dull. At other times, it appears in uncritical borrowing from cultural ideas or popular trends that may seem harmless but lack biblical grounding. Over time, such small compromises can reshape a pastor's worldview and erode the church's foundation. For this reason, the pursuit of theological growth is essential. Vanhoozer and Strachan underscores this truth: "The local church is the place where God intends theological understanding to be nurtured and shown to be wise in its practical outworking."[46] His reminder reframes theology as more than classroom learning; it is the daily lifeblood of pastoral leadership, shaping sermons, counseling conversations, and discipleship.

Paul's warning to Timothy speaks powerfully into our own age: "For the time is coming when people will not endure sound teaching, but having itching ears they will accumulate for themselves teachers to suit their own passions" (2 Tim 4:3, ESV). This reality is evident today, when many are drawn to teachers who echo personal preferences rather than proclaim God's truth. In such a climate, the pastor must remain deeply anchored in Scripture. R. Albert Mohler calls pastors to embrace their calling as "theologians-in-residence,"[47] recognizing that shepherds are entrusted with the task of cultivating

---

46   Kevin J. Vanhoozer and Owen Strachan, *The Pastor as Public Theologian: Reclaiming a Lost Vision* (Grand Rapids: Baker Academic, 2015), 132.

47   R. Albert Mohler Jr., *He Is Not Silent: Preaching in a Postmodern World* (Chicago: Moody, 2008), 69.

conviction and clarity within the local church. This responsibility is not simply about guarding doctrine in the abstract but about ensuring that truth is lived out and applied for the health of Christ's people.

Theological growth also strengthens a pastor's confidence in the authority of Scripture. Paul Henebury reminds us of the danger of careless interpretation: "This is no reason to abandon normative Grammatical-Historical hermeneutics and introduce another set of hermeneutics which will play fast and loose with the words of these texts."[48] His caution highlights the importance of a consistent and faithful hermeneutic, for when Scripture is handled lightly, both teaching and shepherding suffer. Pastors who take the authority of God's Word seriously will approach it with reverence, study it diligently, and proclaim it boldly. Their confidence will not rest in their own wisdom but in the sufficiency of God's revelation. Such commitment protects both pastor and congregation from being shaped more by cultural winds than by biblical truth.

In this way, theological growth is an act of both humility and love. Pastors who continue to grow in doctrine demonstrate that they themselves remain students of the Word, willingly submitting to its authority. Their study is not aimed at novelty but at nourishing their people with truth that endures. In times of cultural upheaval or congregational unrest, it is the pastor-theologian who provides steadiness, offering revelation rather than reaction, nourishment rather than trend. A shepherd who continues to deepen in theology will not only endure but also lead others to maturity. His growth equips him to guide with wisdom, correct with gentleness, and encourage with confidence, showing the church that truth is not fragile but unshakable.

---

48 Paul Henebury, "Answering the 95 Theses against Dispensationalism, Part 7," *SharperIron* (July 2010), https://sharperiron.org/article/answering-95-theses-against-dispensationalism-part-7

Pastoral Endurance Requires Doctrinal Depth

The calling to pastoral ministry is not a static role but a lifelong pursuit of growth and maturity. A pastor who ceases to learn eventually places both himself and his congregation in danger, for a stagnant shepherd cannot lead a flourishing flock. Ministry is not sustained by willpower alone; it is sustained by deep engagement with the Word of God. Doctrinal depth strengthens the pastor to endure through seasons of trial and equips him to lead with clarity in moments of uncertainty. In this way, endurance in ministry is inseparably linked to theological growth, for the pastor's strength to continue rests on his grasp of God's truth.

Theological education must therefore be understood not as an accumulation of data but as a process of transformation. Through careful study, the pastor develops discernment, cultivates wisdom, and is conformed more closely to the character of Christ. Learning strengthens preaching, enriches counseling, and deepens prayer. Far from distracting from ministry, theological study equips the pastor for it. This is why Paul reminded Timothy that the Scriptures are able to make him "complete, equipped for every good work" (2 Tim 3:17, ESV). A pastor who keeps growing in knowledge and wisdom demonstrates that his confidence rests not in himself but in the sufficiency of God's Word.

John Piper captures the connection between theology and devotion: "Education about God precedes and serves exultation in God. Learning truth precedes loving truth. Right reflection on God precedes right affection for God.... Good theology is the foundation of great doxology."[49] In this statement, Piper reminds pastors that theological study is not cold or lifeless but an act of worship. To learn about God rightly is to be moved to love Him more deeply. A pastor who embraces this vision will find that his own delight in God

---

49   John Piper, "Education about God Precedes and Serves Exultation in God," *Desiring God* (1996), https://www.desiringgod.org

increases as his knowledge of God expands, and this joy will over-
flow into his preaching, teaching, and leadership. In this way, doctrinal growth sustains not only endurance but also joy in the work
of ministry.

This emphasis on doctrinal certainty has long been affirmed
throughout church history. Martin Luther insisted, "The preacher
must be sure of his doctrine. If he is not, he had better hold his
tongue."[50] Charles Spurgeon warned against preaching devoid of
Christ, saying, "If a man can preach one sermon without mentioning
Christ's name in it, it ought to be his last."[51] Both men understood
that the preacher's effectiveness is tied directly to his faithfulness in
declaring the truth of God's Word. Their conviction was that endurance is not found in cleverness or popularity but in steadfast proclamation of the gospel. These voices remind modern pastors that doctrinal growth is essential for long-term fruitfulness.

The enduring relevance of doctrine is also emphasized by contemporary theologians. John Frame succinctly writes, "Theology is
application."[52] In this simple phrase, Frame underscores that doctrine is not abstract theory, but the living truth of God applied to life
and ministry. Doctrinal study, therefore, is not merely academic but
intensely practical, shaping how a pastor prays, counsels, preaches,
and endures hardship. To grow in theology is to grow in the ability
to shepherd well. A pastor who takes doctrine seriously not only safe-
guards his own soul but also provides stability for his congregation,
ensuring that they too are equipped to remain steadfast in the faith.

Dr. Thomas Pittman explains that educated pastors contrib-
ute to stronger church structures, understanding pastoral care,

---

50   Martin Luther, "Sermon to the Princes of the Empire, June 1530," in *Luther's Works*,
     ed. Jaroslav Pelikan, vol. 44 (Philadelphia: Fortress, 1966), 289.

51   Charles Haddon Spurgeon, *Sermons Preached and Revised by C. H. Spurgeon*, vol. 2
     (London: Passmore & Alabaster, 1861), 143.

52   John M. Frame, *The Doctrine of the Knowledge of God* (Phillipsburg, NJ: Presbyterian
     & Reformed, 1987), 43.

communication, and resilience in adversity.[53] Such leaders demonstrate that theological growth produces not only endurance for themselves but also stability and growth for the entire church.

Growing into Fruitfulness

The goal of theological growth is never the accumulation of knowledge alone but the cultivation of lasting fruit in ministry. Knowledge without transformation produces pride, but knowledge joined with godliness results in flourishing. Paul's prayer for the Colossians reflects this balance beautifully: he asks that they be "filled with the knowledge of his will in all spiritual wisdom and understanding, so as to walk in a manner worthy of the Lord, fully pleasing to him, bearing fruit in every good work and increasing in the knowledge of God" (Col 1:9–10, ESV). Notice that Paul ties knowledge and fruit together—growth in understanding is meant to lead to growth in living. For pastors, this truth is crucial, because their fruitfulness in ministry depends upon the depth of their roots in God's Word.

Jesus reinforced this connection between depth and fruit in the parable of the sower (Matt 13:1–23). He warned that seed falling on rocky ground quickly sprang up but withered away because it had no depth of soil. By contrast, seed planted in good soil produced fruit in abundance. The lesson is unmistakable: true, enduring fruit requires deep roots. In pastoral ministry, charisma or innovation may produce temporary excitement, but only a deep foundation in Scripture will sustain a congregation through the trials of life. Pastors who continually cultivate theological growth are like farmers who prepare the soil well, ensuring that lasting fruit will follow. Fruitfulness in ministry must therefore be measured not by outward success but by faithfulness. Jesus declared, "By this my Father is glorified, that you

---

53 Thomas Pittman, "A Lifelong Learner," in *Vital Signs of a Healthy Pastor*, eds. David Deets and Richard Bargas (Grandville, MI: IFCA International, 2025), 59.

bear much fruit and so prove to be my disciples" (John 15:8, ESV). Fruit that glorifies God is not always visible in numbers or immediate results; it often appears in steady discipleship, quiet acts of love, and generational faithfulness. A pastor who abides in Christ and teaches his people to do the same will see the fruit of transformed character and deepened maturity within the congregation. This fruit, though sometimes slow in its appearance, testifies to the power of God's Word at work. Faithfulness, not flash, is the measure of true pastoral success.

Theological growth also shapes the culture of the local church. When a pastor models humility in learning and demonstrates eagerness to keep growing, the congregation is encouraged to pursue the same. A learning pastor creates a learning church. In such an environment, questions are welcomed, Scripture is explored, and discipleship becomes part of the congregation's DNA. As Pittman further notes, pastors who devote themselves to continued study create stronger church cultures that are equipped to endure adversity and flourish in ministry.[54]

Generational fruitfulness is perhaps the clearest sign of enduring ministry. A faithful pastor not only serves his present flock but also equips future leaders and disciples. Paul's instruction to Timothy highlights this principle: "what you have heard from me in the presence of many witnesses entrust to faithful men, who will be able to teach others also" (2 Tim. 2:2, ESV). Fruitful ministry plants seeds for future growth, passing on truth from one generation to the next. Families are strengthened, young believers are discipled, and leaders are raised up who will carry the gospel forward. This multiplication of faith and faithfulness is the natural result of theological depth. The pastor who grows continually in Christ does more than endure; he leaves a legacy of fruitfulness that glorifies God for generations to come.

---

54   Pittman, "A Lifelong Learner", 59.

The Pastor-Scholar's Legacy and Model

The enduring fruit of pastoral ministry is measured not in public acclaim or temporary recognition but in consistent faithfulness to Christ over time. The pastor who endures demonstrates that ministry is not about achieving fame but about serving God and His people with humility. Paul reminded Timothy of this generational vision when he wrote, "what you have heard from me in the presence of many witnesses entrust to faithful men who will be able to teach others also" (2 Tim 2:2, ESV). This instruction highlights the principle of multiplication. A pastor who faithfully teaches others ensures that his ministry outlives him, bearing fruit in the next generation of disciples and leaders. Such faithfulness creates a legacy that blesses the church long after his personal labor is complete.

The model of the pastor-scholar flows directly from this principle. He is not defined by the possession of advanced academic degrees but by a spirit of devotion and diligence in handling the Word of God. His study is not intended to impress but to equip him for shepherding. Richard Baxter captured this responsibility when he warned, "Take heed to yourselves, lest your example contradict your doctrine."[55] A pastor who studies carefully but lives carelessly undermines his own ministry. By contrast, the pastor-scholar who allows his private devotion to fuel his public faithfulness models a life of integrity before God and His people. His theology and his practice are united in a way that strengthens the credibility of his message.

Lifelong learning must therefore be seen as part of ministry itself. To be a faithful shepherd is to be a continual student of God's truth. The pastor who reads, studies, reflects, and meditates is not pursuing knowledge for prestige but for the sake of service. His growth equips him to feed the flock and to guide them with wisdom and grace. Over time, his persistence in learning becomes a stabilizing presence for his

---

55 Richard Baxter, *The Reformed Pastor* (1656; repr., Carlisle, PA: Banner of Truth, 1974), 67.

congregation. When members see their pastor continuing to learn, they are encouraged to imitate that example, cultivating their own hunger for truth. The result is not simply a well-educated leader but a community shaped by the steady influence of a growing shepherd.

In today's complex cultural environment, the pastor-scholar also serves as a guide for navigating difficult questions and challenges. He does not retreat from culture but engages it through the lens of Scripture. He listens carefully, discerns wisely, and speaks clearly. This requires the heart of a shepherd and the mind of a theologian. By serving as both apologist and counselor, he equips his people to think biblically and live faithfully. In doing so, he embodies the New Testament model of ministry—rooted in truth, expressed in love, and committed to endurance. The impact of such a pastor is not measured by momentary attention but by long-term transformation in the lives of those he disciples.

The lasting contribution of pastor-scholars throughout history illustrates this principle. Leaders such as Martin Luther, John Calvin, and Charles Spurgeon endured because they were grounded in the truth of God's Word. Luther insisted on the certainty of doctrine, Spurgeon proclaimed Christ with unrelenting conviction, and each modeled the integration of study and ministry. Their example demonstrates that the pastor who remains committed to learning not only sustains his own ministry but also blesses generations after him. A faithful pastor-scholar leaves behind more than sermons and writings; he leaves behind disciples who know, love, and live the Word of God. This is the enduring legacy of one who has chosen to be both shepherd and student all his days.

The Pastor-Scholar in Practice

The vision of the pastor-scholar must not remain abstract; it must be lived out in the rhythms of daily ministry. Paul describes this dynamic in 2 Corinthians 4:1–2: "Therefore, having this ministry by the mercy of God, we do not lose heart. But we have renounced disgraceful, underhanded ways. We refuse to practice cunning or to tamper with God's word, but by the open statement of the truth we would commend ourselves to everyone's conscience in the sight of God" (ESV). Here Paul connects ministry integrity with clarity in teaching. The faithful pastor not only studies but also embodies what he learns, allowing doctrine and conduct to work together for the glory of God.

For such a vision to become reality, the pastor must establish intentional patterns that sustain theological growth. Good intentions alone cannot carry a ministry forward; structure and discipline are necessary. Donald Whitney highlights the value of these rhythms, noting that spiritual disciplines such as Bible intake, prayer, and meditation are essential to long-term vitality in the Christian life.[56] In the same way, pastors who build consistent habits of reading, reflection, and study are better prepared to serve their congregations. Their intentionality ensures that learning does not remain sporadic but becomes a way of life. Over time, these steady disciplines yield fruit in sermons, counseling, and leadership that are both thoughtful and deeply biblical.

In addition to personal study, the pastor-scholar must also be committed to equipping others. Ezra provides a powerful model of this in the Old Testament: "For Ezra had set his heart to study the Law of the LORD, and to do it and to teach his statutes and rules in Israel" (Ezra 7:10, ESV). Ezra's example shows the natural progression of a faithful teacher—study, application, and teaching. The pastor who follows this pattern not only grows in knowledge himself but also shares that knowledge for the good of the flock. This multiplication of wisdom ensures that the church is not dependent on one leader alone but is strengthened by a growing body of disciples.

---

56 Donald S. Whitney, *Spiritual Disciplines for the Christian Life* (Colorado Springs: NavPress, 1991), 121–22.

In this way, the pastor-scholar plants seeds that will continue to bear fruit in future generations.

The practice of the pastor-scholar also includes engaging with contemporary challenges. The world presents new ethical, cultural, and theological questions in every generation, and pastors cannot ignore them. Instead, they must guide their people through such questions with the light of Scripture. David Dockery encourages pastors to see their intellectual development as a spiritual discipline pursued for the sake of service rather than status.[57] This perspective frees pastors from the pressure to be experts in every field while reminding them that they are responsible to lead with discernment. By engaging culture biblically and thoughtfully, the pastor-scholar demonstrates that God's truth is sufficient for all of life's complexities.

The consistent practice of the pastor-scholar ultimately blesses the church by shaping a culture of conviction and learning. In a time when many are drawn to charisma or novelty, the enduring influence of the faithful pastor is found in his steady teaching and consistent example. His sermons are rich because his study is deep, and his counsel is wise because his heart is saturated with Scripture. Congregations led by such pastors become stable, resilient, and mission-focused. The impact of his practice is not seen only in the present but also in the lives of those who are equipped to lead after him. The enduring pastor-scholar, though often unnoticed by the world, is used by God to nourish His people for generations.

Conclusion: Pressing On for the Sake of Christ

The Christian life, and especially pastoral ministry, is a race that requires endurance. The apostle Paul captures this truth in Philippians

---

57 David S. Dockery, "The Pastor as Theologian: A Biblical Paradigm," in *The Pastor as Theologian and Scholar: Essays in Honor of John R. Ryan*, ed. *David S. Dockery* (Nashville: Broadman & Holman, 2007), 27.

3:12–14: "Not that I have already obtained this or am already perfect, but I press on to make it my own, because Christ Jesus has made me his own. Brothers, I do not consider that I have made it my own. But one thing I do: forgetting what lies behind and straining forward to what lies ahead, I press on toward the goal for the prize of the upward call of God in Christ Jesus" (ESV). Ministry, like discipleship, is not static; it is an ongoing pursuit of Christ. The pastor who endures demonstrates that his ultimate motivation is not recognition or comfort but faithfulness to the Lord who has called him. By fixing his eyes on Jesus, the shepherd finds strength to continue, even when challenges are great.

This posture of pressing on transforms not only the pastor but also the congregation. A shepherd who grows in knowledge and maturity creates an atmosphere where learning is valued and spiritual growth is expected. His example becomes contagious, inspiring others to deepen their own walk with Christ. A culture of growth within the church begins with the pastor's commitment to be a lifelong learner. When members see their pastor humbly continuing to study and pursue wisdom, they are encouraged to do the same. In this way, pastoral endurance fosters congregational fruitfulness, as the flock follows the example of their shepherd.

In God's providence, the digital age has given pastors access to a wealth of resources that can encourage this lifelong learning. Online theological libraries, discussion forums, and global networks make it possible to engage with voices and scholarship from around the world. These tools, however, must be used with discernment, for not all voices are equally faithful to Scripture. When stewarded wisely, such resources can enrich study, sharpen discernment, and enhance pastoral ministry. Technology is never a substitute for the Scriptures, but it can be a helpful servant to the pastor committed to growing in the Word. The wise pastor uses every available means to deepen his understanding so that he may strengthen the church.

Theological education is therefore not an institutional luxury but a pastoral imperative. Paul urged Timothy to "do your best to present yourself to God as one approved, a worker who has no need to be ashamed, rightly handling the word of truth" (2 Tim 2:15, ESV). This charge remains binding on pastors today. A shepherd who continues to learn is better prepared to protect the flock from error, to nourish them with sound doctrine, and to lead them with wisdom. Far from distracting from ministry, ongoing study fuels it. The pastor who grows in knowledge and depth becomes not only more effective in his present calling but also more faithful in leaving a legacy for the future.

Let us then press on as pastor-scholars, not for prestige but for the glory of Christ and the good of His church. Let us plant ourselves firmly by the streams of truth, that in every season we may bear fruit that endures. By nourishing our own souls, we prepare ourselves to nourish the flock of God. By pursuing wisdom, we glorify the God of wisdom. And by remaining steadfast to the end, we may finish the race with joy, having held fast to the Word of life, and hear the words, "Well done, good and faithful servant" (Matt 25:23, ESV).

8

STEADY GROWTH:
THE IMPORTANCE OF
CONSISTENCY

Aaron Valdizan

Any tree with access to adequate soil, water, and sunlight will grow. Although that growth may seem slow—only a few inches a year for some trees—it is steady, consistent growth that can continue for centuries or even millennia. Similarly, being consistent in one's spiritual life and ministry is a key element for a long-lasting ministry. Spiritual and ministerial consistency is essential for perseverance in ministry because consistency is not only rooted in God's nature but is also exemplified and commanded in God's Word.

Divine Consistency

The importance of consistency in Christian life and ministry stems ultimately from God's nature. The divine attribute of immutability means that God's attributes and character never change. God is perfectly consistent. In Malachi 3:6 God declares, "For I the LORD do not change." The psalmist also says to God, "you are the same, and your years have no end" (Ps 102:27). This attribute can be seen in the New Testament as well. James states that with God "there is no variation or shadow due to change" (Jas 1:17), and the author of Hebrews

93

speaks of God's "unchangeable character" (Heb 6:17). Thus, we see from both testaments that Yahweh is characterized by consistency, and He is its ultimate example. His consistency can also be seen in the orderly nature of the universe. We can predict when the sun will rise or set on any given day because God made the times, seasons, and heavenly bodies to function in consistent patterns (cf. Gen 8:22).

Because God is unchanging and thoroughly consistent in all His ways, He is also faithful, and we can trust Him fully. Reagan Rose notes, "God's faithfulness—or we might say His consistency—is the basis of our trust in Him. We trust that He will follow through because of His unchanging nature and perfect record of doing what He says He will do."[58] Paul also states, "if we are faithless, he remains faithful—for he cannot deny himself" (2 Tim 2:13). Grudem highlights the importance of God's consistency when he writes,

> If God is not unchanging, then the whole basis of our faith begins to fall apart, and our understanding of the universe begins to unravel. This is because our faith and hope and knowledge all ultimately depend on a *person* who is *infinitely worthy of truth*—because he is *absolutely* and *eternally* unchanging in his being, perfections, purposes, and promises.[59]

As the most consistent being in the universe, God sets the standard for consistency that we should strive for in our lives and ministries. Consistency is one of many attributes of God that we should emulate, and it will be seen that God's Word also commands us to be consistent.

---

58   Reagan Rose, "Why You're Inconsistent (And What to Do About It)," *Redeeming Productivity*, 30 April 2024, https://www.redeemingproductivity.com/why-youre-inconsistent-and-what-to-do-about-it/.

59   Wayne Grudem, *Systematic Theology: An Introduction to Biblical Doctrine* (Grand Rapids: Zondervan, 1994), 168.

Biblical Examples of Consistency

Scripture tells us of several individuals who lived exemplarily consistent lives. Daniel is most notable. Taken from his homeland as an exile when just a youth, Daniel and his friends faced many challenges to their faith in Yahweh. Upon arrival in Babylon, their conviction to obey God's law was challenged when the king wanted them to eat the same food as himself, which included meats forbidden by the Mosaic law and foods that had been offered to idols. When put in this potentially life-threatening situation, Daniel showed consistency in his conviction to keep God's law: "But Daniel resolved that he would not defile himself with the king's food, or with the wine he drank. Therefore he asked the chief of the eunuchs to allow him not to defile himself" (Dan 1:8).

Even when the government official responsible for him hesitated to accommodate Daniel's convictions, Daniel remained consistent and didn't back down. Instead of giving in, he respectfully proposed a trial period that would enable him and his friends to stay true to their convictions for at least ten more days (Dan 1:12–13). The rest of that story recounts how God rewarded the faithfulness of Daniel and his friends by not only making them healthier than the other youths who were eating the king's choice food, but also by giving them wisdom and favor with their masters. The king even made them his most trusted advisors (Dan 1:14–20).

Daniel was not only consistent in his convictions but also in his prayer life. When Daniel and his friends were in danger of being executed by an enraged Nebuchadnezzar, his response was to meet with his friends and pray together for the Lord to have compassion on them and spare their lives (Dan 2:17–18). His immediate response to impending death was to pray!

Many years and an empire later, during the reign of Darius the Mede, Daniel's consistency was used against him by his enemies. His praying daily was so well-known that his political rivals used it to get him in trouble. When they couldn't find any corruption to accuse him of, they manufactured a way to use his faith to kill him. They said, "We shall not find any ground for complaint against this Daniel unless we find it in connection with the law of his God" (Dan 6:5). Daniel was so consistent in his convictions and prayer habits that the conspirators based their entire plan to destroy him on that consistency.

When they convinced the king to make a law prohibiting his subjects from praying to anyone other than himself for thirty days, Daniel remained consistent in his convictions and daily prayer. Daniel responded as follows: "When Daniel knew that the document had been signed, he went to his house where he had windows in his upper chamber open toward Jerusalem. He got down on his knees three times a day and prayed and gave thanks before his God, as he had done previously" (Dan 6:10). His response was not to respond; he continued doing what he'd always done. He remained consistent in his daily prayer practice regardless of what it might cost him.

The familiar story then continues with Daniel being thrown into the lions' den, God saving Daniel from being devoured, and Darius proclaiming the greatness of Daniel's God in an official decree (Dan 6:25–27). God then rewards Daniel's consistency by giving him great success in the court of Darius and later of Cyrus (Dan 6:28). Tracing these events in Daniel's life has shown that Daniel was consistent in his spiritual convictions and personal prayer life from his youth and throughout his life. God rewarded his consistency by giving him one of the longest and most fruitful ministries, spanning two empires over seventy years. May we all strive for such lifelong consistency and ministry longevity!

It should come as no surprise that Jesus also stands out in Scripture as the ultimate example of consistency. As God in human form, Jesus perfectly reflects God's perfect consistency. Thus, the author of Hebrews tells us, "Jesus Christ is the same yesterday and today and forever" (Heb 13:8). Like Daniel, his life modeled consistent prayer. Luke 5:16 notes, "But he would withdraw to desolate places and pray." Even to this day, Jesus consistently intercedes for His people:

"but he holds his priesthood permanently, because he continues forever. Consequently, he is able to save to the uttermost those who draw near to God through him, since he always lives to make intercession for them" (Heb 7:24–25). Paul also affirms Jesus' continuous intercession when he writes, "Who is to condemn? Christ Jesus is the one who died—more than that, who was raised—who is at the right hand of God, who indeed is interceding for us" (Rom 8:34).

Jesus was consistent in everything He did while on this planet. He was consistent in obedience, only doing the will of His father. He said, "And he who sent me is with me. He has not left me alone, for I always do the things that are pleasing to him." (John 8:29). He was also consistent in humility, as Paul so eloquently put it, saying that Christ "who, though he was in the form of God, did not count equality with God a thing to be grasped, but emptied himself, by taking the form of a servant, being born in the likeness of men. And being found in human form, he humbled himself by becoming obedient to the point of death, even death on a cross" (Phil 2:6–8). His ways and deeds as recounted throughout the Gospels further testify to Christ's consistent humility. Let us strive for the kind of consistency we see in Daniel and Christ.

Commands for Consistency

Consistency is not only part of who God is and a trait modeled by select individuals throughout Scripture, but it is also commanded in the New Testament. Scripture commands us to be consistent in our spiritual lives and ministries.

Spiritual consistency is often connected to the spiritual discipline of prayer. As shown above, the most prevalent examples of consistency in the lives of Daniel and Jesus were related to prayer. Similarly, the New Testament commands about consistency are also often linked to prayer. There can be no clearer call to consistency in prayer than Paul's command that we "pray without ceasing" (1 Thess 5:17). He gives a similar command to the church in Rome when he says they should be "constant in prayer" (Rom 12:12) and further commands the church at Colossae to "Continue steadfastly in prayer" (Col 4:2). It's fitting prayer should be the starting point for spiritual consistency because prayer is how we ask the Lord to empower us to be consistent in every area of our lives. Consistent prayer is indeed essential for a consistent life and ministry.

James links spiritual consistency to faith when he says that the one who doubts God when praying is "unstable in all his ways" (Jas 1:8). Believers must pray consistently and with faith in our perfectly consistent Lord to give us consistency in all we do. Thankfully, we can pray for consistency with full confidence that the Lord will answer because the Holy Spirit enables us to be consistent. The fruit of the Spirit listed in Galatians 5:22–23 includes faithfulness, which is directly linked to consistency. As those in whom the Holy Spirit dwells, every believer has the Spirit-empowered ability to live and serve consistently.

In addition to prayer, the author of Hebrews tells us to be consistent in faith and fellowship, saying, "Let us hold fast the confession of our hope without wavering, for he who promised is faithful. And let us consider how to stir up one another to love and good works, not neglecting to meet together, as is the habit of some, but encouraging one another, and all the more as you see the Day drawing near" (Heb 10:23–25). It's not only in the prayer closet but also among the local body of believers that we're to be consistent and stimulate one another toward greater consistency. God has designed the church community to be a means of accountability for improving spiritual consistency.

Ministerial consistency is also commanded in Scripture. Paul tells the Corinthians to be consistent in ministering when he writes, "be steadfast, immovable, always abounding in the work of the Lord, knowing that in the Lord your labor is not in vain" (1 Cor 15:58). To the Galatians he also commands consistency in ministry through a negative command: "And let us not grow weary of doing good, for in due season we will reap, if we do not give up" (Gal 6:9). Paul also says to Titus, "Show yourself in all respects to be a model of good works, and in your teaching show integrity, dignity, and sound speech that cannot be condemned, so that an opponent may be put to shame, having nothing evil to say about us" (Titus 2:7–8). And he charges Timothy to be consistent in doctrine: "Follow the pattern of the sound words that you have heard from me, in the faith and love that are in Christ Jesus" (2 Tim 1:13). Consistency is essential to biblical ministry.

Longevity from Consistency Exemplified

We've seen that consistency is important for our spiritual lives and ministries because it's part of God's nature and is both exemplified and commanded in Scripture. But how does consistency lead to ministry longevity? An example from modern history is helpful for seeing the relationship between consistency and longevity.

American missionary Adoniram Judson stands out as a man characterized by a consistency learned through suffering. The first fifteen years of his ministry in early nineteenth-century Burma were marked by one extreme tragedy after another. During that time, he spent twenty-one months in a Burmese "death prison" where he endured beatings and torture. His first wife and all their children succumbed to disease during those first years of ministry. Nevertheless, after recovering from the deaths of his entire family, he came out of that dark time as a man of great consistency. This was mostly clearly observable in his prayer life. Edward, a son by his second wife, described his prayer habits as follows:

> He was a man of prayer. His habit was to walk while engaged in private prayer. One who knew him most intimately says that "His best and freest time for meditation and prayer was while walking rapidly in the open air. He, however, attended to the duty in his room, and so well was this peculiarity understood that when the children heard a somewhat heavy,

quick, but well-measured tread, up and down the room, they would say, 'Papa is praying.'"[60]

Among his few belongings, a scrap of paper was discovered on which Judson had written, "Whatever others do, let my life be a life of prayer."[61] In a manner similar to that of Jonathan Edwards' "Resolutions," Judson had written a list for himself of "Rules for Life" that he reviewed regularly in order to foster consistency in his Christian walk. The rules included the following: Rise with the sun; Be diligent in secret prayer, every morning and evening; Read a certain portion of Burman every day, Sundays excepted; Have the Scriptures and some devotional book in constant reading.[62] Judson was consistent in prayer and devotional time.

Judson was also consistent in humility. Knowing he had a natural tendency toward pride, he went to great lengths to maintain his humility. For example, he declined an honorary doctorate from Brown University in 1823 and even wrote letters to publishers, requesting they not designate him as a doctor in their publications about him.[63] His son commented on how difficult it was to write his biography because he'd destroyed nearly all the letters he'd received during his lifetime, which included many letters of appreciation and praise for his accomplishments. His son remarks, "He seemed determined that his friends should have no material with which to construct eulogiums. He wanted to do his work and then forget all about it and have every one else also forget it."[64]

---

60 Edward Judson, *The Life of Adoniram Judson* (New York: Anson D. F. Randolph & Company, 1883), 311.

61 Judson, *The Life of Adoniram Judson*, 314.

62 Judson, *The Life of Adoniram Judson*, 315–16.

63 Judson, *The Life of Adoniram Judson*, 319–20.

64 Judson, *The Life of Adoniram Judson*, 320.

Through his consistent hard work and the Lord's enabling, Adoniram Judson produced several Burmese gospel tracts, a Burmese grammar, the Burmese-English part of the first Burmese dictionary, and the first translation of the Bible into Burmese, which he translated from the original languages. On top of his translation and writing ministry, he was preaching regularly and discipling local believers as well. His consistency in life and ministry led to a long and fruitful ministry. He died after ministering faithfully for thirty-five years in a land where most Western missionaries barely lasted a few years, often dying from tropical diseases within months of arrival. Judson's life and ministry remind us of the importance of consistency for ministry longevity.

Conclusion

The consistent growth of a tree over time reminds us that spiritual and ministerial consistency are necessary for persevering in ministry. Such consistency is inherent in God's nature and is available to us through the empowerment of the Holy Spirit as part of the fruit of the Spirit. Scripture has given us examples of the kind of consistency that pleases God and leads to fruitful ministry. Commands for spiritual and ministerial consistency also pervade the New Testament.

If you struggle with consistency in your spiritual walk or ministry, it's never too late to seek God's help in the matter. Even those who naturally tend toward consistency can be easily thrown off course. Let us all regularly seek the Lord's gracious enabling to maintain consistency in our spiritual lives and ministries so that those ministries may grow steadily in His time.

9

SOWING SEEDS: PREPARING THE NEXT GENERATION

David L. Burggraff

Where do trees come from? The answer is so obvious to every-one—even to children—that it seems foolish to ask the question. But let's rephrase the question: where did trees originally come from? Now things are getting complicated and controversial—even for scientists, evolutionary botanists, and plant biophysicists. In the introduction of this book, we read the honest admission of the lack of definiteness as to the origin of the nearly sixty thousand known tree species by evolutionist Elizabeth Stacy from the University of Hawaii:

> But we know next to nothing about how they got here…. Trees form the backbone of our forests, and are ecologi-cally and economically important, yet we don't know much about how speciation happens in trees.[65]

---

65   Quoted in Marlene Cimon's article, "Tracing the Evolution of Forest Trees," National Science Foundation, November 7, 2014, http://www.nsf.gov. I first came across this quote while reading the chapter "Taught by a Forest of Trees" in Stephen Davey's insightful book, *In Living Color* (Cary, NC: Charity House, 2020). The chapter on trees is both interesting and informative, as is the entire book that demonstrates the creative handiwork of God. I highly recommend his book.

Trees, simply put, puzzle evolutionists.[66] Stephen Davey writes," "For them, the origin of wood is unknown and they can't quite figure out how, where, and when the first tree came to be. Believers, on the other hand, accept the eyewitness account of God, who informs us that trees were created by His verbal and creative command on the third day of the creation week."[67]

We read in the creation account, "And God said, 'Let the earth sprout vegetation, plants yielding seed, and fruit trees bearing fruit in which is their seed, each according to its kind, on the earth.' And it was so" (Gen1:11). There is our answer to the question—where did trees originally come from? The first trees, along with other plant life, came into existence on the third day of the creation week as fully mature trees already bearing fruit, which contained seeds for reproduction each according to their kind. God was speaking into existence a completely developed creation. This is referred to as *ex nihilo, fiat, de novo* creation.[68] Living things were created ready to reproduce, including plant life (Gen 1:11–13), animals (Gen 1:20–25), and humans (Gen 1:26–30).

Trees: Marvels of God's Creation

Science can't explain *where* the first trees came from, but researchers can tell us a great deal about *what* they've learned through recent

---

66   For an attempted explanation, which shows how evolutionists merely hypothesize, see plant biophysicist Esa Tystjarvi's article (http://www.quora.com/How-did-the-growth-of-trees-and-plants-happen-on-Earth). Of note is the speculation throughout his explanation. Admittedly, when it comes to origins, he and other evolutionists can only honestly offer "we do not know," or "probably," or the matter "is not yet understood very well."

67   Stephen Davey, *In Living Color*, 58–59.

68   The explanation of creation that best fits the biblical doctrine of divine creation is *fiat creationism*, which contends that God created the universe by *fiat* (or decree, declaration), and out of nothing (*ex nihilo*). Also, God created all things mature (*de novo*) and functional, with the appearance of age.

studies. Trees are full of surprises! Here are a few facts that help us see them in a whole new light:

- *They can live for thousands of years.* The oldest known tree is a bristlecone pine in California, estimated to be over 4,800 years old. It was already centuries old when the pyramids were built!

- *They affect the weather.* Forests release water vapor through their leaves in a process called transpiration, which helps form clouds and even influences rainfall patterns.

- *They're natural air conditioners.*[69] A single large tree can have the cooling effect of ten air conditioning units, thanks to the shade it casts and the moisture it releases.

- *They're the world's air purifiers.*[70] While God designed most living things to breathe oxygen and breathe out carbon dioxide as a waste product, trees absorb carbon dioxide and breathe out oxygen. Without trees, we can't survive!

---

69 By shading surfaces and releasing water vapor through transpiration, trees lower urban temperatures, which also helps reduce the formation of ground-level ozone—a major air pollutant.

70 Trees improve air quality in several powerful ways:

- *Absorbing pollutants*: Leaves have tiny pores called *stomata* that take in gases like carbon monoxide (CO), nitrogen dioxide (NO_2), sulfur dioxide (SO_2), and ozone. Once inside, these gases are broken down or stored in the tree's tissues.

- *Trapping particulates*: Dust, smoke, and other fine particles stick to leaves and bark. When it rains, these particles are washed off into the soil, reducing what we breathe in.

- *They help clean our water.* [71] Trees also play a crucial role in water purification.

- *Their rings are like time machines.* By studying the rings of a tree, scientists can uncover not just its age, but details about historical climates, volcanic eruptions, and even ancient droughts.

- *They're designed to ensure reproduction.* A single tree is capable of producing vast amounts of seeds enabling reproduction of itself.

- *They communicate with each other.* Through underground fungal networks (sometimes called the "Wood Wide Web"), trees can share nutrients and chemical signals—warning neighbors about pests or drought conditions.

It's pretty amazing—trees don't just stand there looking pretty; they're working full-time to keep our environment stable, breathable, and drinkable. But it's the last two facts above, concerning the reproduction and communication of trees, which are of interest to this study.

First, how many seeds does a tree produce to ensure the reproduction of itself? That depends on the species of tree—some are modest, others are downright overachievers.

---

71   Trees play a major role in water purification:

- *Filtering runoff:* Tree roots and surrounding soil act like a sponge, absorbing rainwater and filtering out pollutants like heavy metals, oils, and pesticides before they reach rivers or groundwater.

- *Reducing erosion:* Roots stabilize soil, preventing sediment from washing into waterways. Less sediment means cleaner streams and healthier aquatic life.

- *Supporting the water cycle:* Through transpiration, trees release water vapor into the air, which contributes to cloud formation and rainfall, helping maintain our local water supplies.

- *Oak trees* can produce thousands of acorns over their lifetime, with mature trees dropping hundreds in a single season.

- *Maple trees* release winged seeds called samaras, and a single tree can produce tens of thousands in a year.

- *Pine trees* generate cones that contain dozens to hundreds of seeds each, and a large pine can produce thousands of them annually.

- On the extreme end, *cottonwood trees* can release millions of tiny seeds each season, carried far and wide by the wind.

So, the range is vast—from a few hundred to several million seeds per year, depending on the tree's size, age, and species. God designed it such that the tree-world doesn't mess around when it comes to giving trees a fighting chance at reproduction.

Seeds, then, are the starting line in a tree's life story—they hold the genetic blueprint of the parent tree and the potential to grow into a whole new organism. Here's how they fit into the cycle:

- *Reproduction*: Seeds are the result of pollination and fertilization. They carry the DNA of the parent(s), ensuring the continuation of the species.

- *Dispersal*: Whether they're carried by wind, water, animals, or gravity, seeds are built to travel. This helps them find a good spot to grow without overcrowding the parent tree.

- *Dormancy*: Some seeds lie in wait, sometimes for months or years, until conditions are just right—like enough moisture, warmth, or sunlight.

- *Germination*: When the environment cooperates, the seed wakes up and begins to grow roots downward and shoots upward, becoming a seedling.

- *Growth*: From there, the seedling matures into a sapling and eventually a full-grown tree, starting the cycle all over again.

So, in essence, a seed is both a messenger from the past and a hope for the future—tiny, but mighty.

Several key factors influence whether a seed successfully germinates, and they fall into two main categories: *external environmental conditions* and *internal seed characteristics*.

External Factors

- *Water*: Seeds need to absorb water in a process called *imbibition*, which activates enzymes and softens the seed coat. Too little water, and the seed stays dormant; too much, and it may rot or suffocate from lack of oxygen.

- *Temperature*: Each species has an optimal temperature range for germination. For many crops, this is around 25–30°C (77–86°F), but some seeds need cooler or warmer conditions.

- *Oxygen*: Seeds require oxygen for cellular respiration, which fuels growth. Poorly aerated or waterlogged soils can limit oxygen availability and hinder germination.

- *Light*: Some seeds need light to germinate (like lettuce), while others prefer darkness (like onions). This trait is species-specific and often tied to natural habitat.

Internal Factors

- *Dormancy*: Some seeds have built-in delays, like hard seed coats or chemical inhibitors, that prevent germination until conditions are just right.

- *Seed viability*: Over time, seeds lose their ability to germinate. Some, like lotus seeds, can last centuries, while others fade within months.[72]

Successful propagation, then, is a delicate dance between a seed's biology (its make-up, characteristics) and the environment (contact with the world).

Second, and perhaps the most fascinating discovery in recent years, is the fact that *trees "communicate."* When we look at a forest, it's easy to see a collection of trees standing tall and separate, each seemingly independent and solitary. However, groundbreaking research has revealed that trees are far from isolated entities. Beneath the forest floor lies a hidden network of connections—an intricate web of roots and fungi that allow trees to "talk" to each other. This system, often referred to as the "*Wood Wide Web*," enables trees to exchange information, share resources, and support one another in ways that were once unimaginable. In essence, researchers are discovering that trees form communities that "talk" to each other, sharing their needs and providing mutual assistance.

Scientists uncovered the hidden world of tree communication through decades of research into mycorrhizal fungi—the thread-like organisms that form symbiotic relationships with tree roots.

One of the pioneers in this field is Dr. Suzanne Simard, a forest ecologist from Canada. In the 1990s, she conducted groundbreaking experiments using radioactive carbon isotopes. She traced how carbon moved from one tree to another through underground fungal networks. Her studies showed that older "mother trees" could send

---

72   https://www.agriculturistmusa.com/factors-affecting-seed-germination/. See also, https://www.biologydiscussion.com/seed/germination/factors-affecting-seed-germina-tion-external-and-internal-factors/15758#google_vignette.

nutrients to younger saplings, especially their own offspring, helping them survive in low-light conditions.[73]

Before we get too caught up about the marvel of trees, it's important to heed the sound advice of researcher Tom Hennigan:

> Now, it's important to remember that forests aren't human or alive in any sense like animals (they lack the "breath" of life, or *nephesh*, according to God's Word). Unfortunately, some current researchers blur the line, imbuing plants with animal or human attributes, such as feelings and consciousness, which they don't have. The science itself is fascinating, without any need to make trees sound human-like.[74]

Communication is happening below our feet. If we could carefully remove the loam at the base of a forest tree, we'd see a root system that spreads out twice as far as the canopy above our heads. This root system reaches depths of one to five feet, depending on the location. More astonishingly, roots may connect directly with the roots of other trees. Trees can distinguish members of their own kind and establish connections with them.

This reality contradicts the old view that woodland trees simply competed in a life-and-death struggle for limited light and nutrients. Though plants do compete in forests, current research suggests that more often, trees may be cooperating and assisting each other. When

---

73   Maria Faith Sarilumab, "The Trees That 'Talk' to Each Other Using Underground Fungal Networks," in *Discover Wild Science*, at https://www.discoverwildscience.com/the-trees-that-talk-to-each-other-using-underground-fungal-networks-1-285018/#google_vignette.

74   Tom Hennigan, "Talking Trees—Secrets of Plant Communication," featured in *Answers Magazine*, April 18, 2018, http://www.answersingenesis.org. Tom Hennigan is a professor of biology at Truett-McConnell University where he teaches organism biology and ecology.

one tree is sick, nearby trees may share nutrients through their roots to help it get well again.[75]

How do plants talk in the soil? They may have several options. Researchers have found evidence that plants are communicating by sound. Though this sounds crazy, vibrations emanating from seedlings in laboratory settings have been detected by special instruments and measured at 220 hertz. In experiments, roots direct other roots to grow toward this low frequency.

Trees also communicate with chemical messages, but they aren't just talking to each other. They talk to their other soil neighbors too. Microorganisms, such as bacteria and fungi, gather water and nutrients that the trees need. So, roots produce nutritious substances, such as sugars and proteins, to attract these organisms. This underground network of root/fungus communication acts like an underground internet. Literally miles of tiny tubes are found within a single cubic foot of soil between two tree roots.[76]

Working together by means of complex communication tools such as sound, chemicals, and electricity, every member in the forest benefits.[77]

75　Hennigan, *Talking Trees*, n.p. For instance, Hennigan writes, "If a lodgepole pine sapling springs up in the shade of a thick forest, older trees somehow sense that it doesn't get enough sunlight to make food for itself, so they may share their bounty. They even change their root structure to open space for saplings."

76　Hennigan, *Talking Trees*, n.p. He notes, "Trees communicate so intensely via these networks that it has been called the 'underground internet'…broadcasting news about drought conditions, predator attacks, and heavy metals contamination."

77　Other researchers observed that when a tree was attacked by pests, it would send chemical distress signals through the mycorrhizal network. Neighboring trees, upon receiving the signal, would boost their own chemical defenses—a kind of early warning system. Essentially, trees connect with each other through a network of thread-like fungi in the soil called *mycorrhizae*. See http://www.discoverwildscience.com/the-trees-that-talk-to-each-other-using-underground-fungal-networks-1-285018/#google_vignette. It's a remarkable system of support and survival that shows forests are less a collection of individuals and more like a *cooperative community*. See http://www.scientificorigin.com/do-trees-talk-to-each-other-the-hidden-language-of-forests.

There's no question these phenomena have been overstated at times and greatly anthropomorphized (described in human-like terms). All forest ecologists see the amazing relationships and interconnections within the forest. As a result, some have called the forest-and-earth biosphere a living organism. But we know from Scripture that a loving Creator is behind them. So how should followers of Christ make sense of these findings?

Trees and Their Seeds: Preparing the Next Generation

From the beginning, God has intended for the propagation of all the good things ("be fruitful and multiply," Gen 1:28) and provided the means to do so across His creation. In the world of plants and trees, propagation is through seed-bearing. For humankind, propagation is through childbearing. In the spiritual realm, we see a propagation of "spiritual life and truth" that is found in the progressive revelation of God's Word—demonstrated in the faith and obedience to what God has revealed in a specific era.

In the Old Testament era, from the time of Adam until Genesis 12, propagation of God's truth and His expectations (i.e., faith and obedience) for mankind came through specific command(s) that God had directed to individuals, expecting those commands to be communicated to the offspring. During the patriarchal period, from the time of Abraham until Moses and the giving of the law, propagation of the covenant promise (i.e., the Abrahamic covenant) was passed down relationally—focusing on parents to children (Gen 12–Exod 20).[78] From the giving of the Mosaic law until the New Testament era, faith and obedience to God was expressed through faith-keeping under the law and the progressive revelation provided by the prophets to the nation of Israel.[79] Of significance for our purposes in this

---

78   Much of the book of Genesis is about families.

79   See Hebrews 11, which recounts examples of those of the OT who lived by faith and pleased God through their faith-obedience.

study, is that "the seed of God's truth" was to be passed on generationally to God's people; the Jewish family unit was paramount for the next generation's (i.e., both children and grandchildren) exposure to and belief in God's Word (Ref. Deut 4:4–9; 4:40; 6:1–9; Ps 127–128; Prov 22:6; 22:17–19; 23:15–19; 22–25).

The New Testament era begins with the first advent of the Messiah revealed in the Gospel accounts. We now encounter two familiar words: *disciple* and *discipleship*. The Gospel of Matthew closes with the final words of our Lord, the Great Commission to the disciples (Matt 28:18–20):

> And Jesus came and said to them [His disciples], "All authority in heaven and earth has been given to me. Go therefore and make disciples of all nations, baptizing them in the name of the Father and of the Son and of the Holy Spirit, teaching them to observe all that I have commanded you. And behold, I am with you always, to the end of the age."

The command to "make disciples" is how we invest in the next generation for the *reproduction and continuation* of our faith. On the basis of His authority, Jesus commissioned His disciples. They (we!) are to "go,"[80] sowing the *seeds* of the gospel of salvation, and "make disciples." This is done by:

- leading them into a faith-based relationship with Christ (i.e., a new birth experience [John 1:12–13; 3:3–7, 16–18]) followed by their identification with Christ through believers' baptism (Acts 2:41).

80　For an explanation of this passage, see Grant R. Osborne, *Matthew: Exegetical Commentary on The New Testament* (Grand Rapids: Zondervan, 2010), esp. 1080.

- teaching them to learn and obey what Christ has commanded them during His ministry, which is later referred to as the "apostles' teaching" (Acts 2:42–44). In essence, Christ's disciples were to reproduce themselves in the lives of others.

But don't overlook the important phrase—*"of all nations"*—in Christ's commission. Consider these words in Eric Geiger and Kevin Peck's book *Designed to Lead* which highlights God's overall plan and the importance of discipleship:

> God has designed the end *and* the means. The end is people from every tribe, tongue, and nation gathered around the throne worshipping Him because they were purchased with the blood of Christ (Rev. 5:9–10). Regardless of what happens this week, what unfolds in the news, the ending has already been made clear: God is redeeming for Himself a people from all peoples.

> The end was made clear in the beginning. God [promised] Abraham saying, "All the nations will be blessed through you" (Gal. 3:8). God told Abraham that people from every nation would have God's righteousness credited to them. At the beginning of the Bible, we find that God is going to pursue all peoples through His chosen people, Israel. At the end of the Bible, we find that God has gathered worshippers from every people group.

> In the middle of the Bible is the means, the command Jesus gave us: "Go, therefore, and make disciples of all nations" (Matt. 28:19). We live in the middle.... The *means* is discipleship. He has commanded us to make disciples of all nations, disciples who will obey everything He commanded.

As Christ is more fully formed in people, the totality of their lives is impacted.[81]

Those of us in the faith know that "making disciples" is our mission—the *means*—for the propagation of the faith, and that the *instrument* that God's people are to use to achieve this is the Word of God (Rom 10:8–17, 2 Tim 3:16–17). Peter tells us as much in his first epistle (1 Pet 1:22–25).

Of interest for our study related to trees is 1 Pet 1:23: "since you have been born again, not of perishable seed but of imperishable, through the living and abiding word of God." The word "seed" (*sporas*), which appears only here in the New Testament, primarily denotes the activity of sowing and was used figuratively of the act of procreation. It also denoted that which was sown, the *seed*.[82] The phrase, "through the word of God," specifies the means or instrument used in regeneration, and according to Peter, the regenerating Word has a dual character; it is "living," actively possessing life, and also "abiding," never obsolete or irrelevant.[83] Peter then authenticates the message—the life-bearing seed—that was brought to his readers with a quotation from Isaiah 40:6–8 that links the New Testament to the Old Testament. As Timothy Miller notes,

> The Word of God from the prophets of the Old Testament to the modern day has the power to bring new life. Isaiah spoke of the power of the Word in his day, Peter confirmed it in his day, and modern believers observe it as well. The

---

81   Eric Geiger and Kevin Peck, *Designed to Lead: The Church and Leadership Development* (Nashville: Broadman & Holman, 2016), 159.

82   D. Edmond Hiebert, *First Peter: An Expositional Commentary* (Chicago: Moody, 1984), 105.

83   Hiebert, *First Peter*, 106–7.

Word of God endures for all time, being applicable in all ages, for it is the voice of the Creator and Redeemer, who calls for himself a people. Thus, to all who have believed in Christ—whether in Peter's day or our own—Peter says, "this [abiding] Word is good news that was preached to you."[84]

Next Generation: Focusing on Discipleship Today

I've been fascinated by the use of words found in Scripture. Notice, I did not say *meaning*, rather the *use* of certain words. For instance, outside the Gospels and Acts, the word *"disciple" essentially vanishes* from the New Testament vocabulary. It's used extensively in the Gospels—*238 times*, to be exact—and appears *twenty-eight times in the book of Acts*, but once you get into the Epistles (Romans through Jude), the term disappears entirely.

Instead, the writers of the Epistles favored terms like *"saints,"* *"brethren,"* and *"believers"* to describe followers of Jesus. Revelation shifts the language dramatically. It leans into vivid imagery and symbolic titles like *"servants,"* *"saints,"* and *"those who overcome"* or *"conquer"* to describe the faithful.

However, in recent times, the noun "disciple" (along with "discipleship") is making a comeback in many churches focused on spiritual formation and intentional living. It underscores the idea of learning from and imitating Jesus, not just believing in Him. The "easy believism" of the mid-to-late twentieth century led to a plethora of books dealing with the true cost of discipleship.[85] It seems that over the past several decades there have been almost as many books on the

---

84 Timothy E. Miller and Bryan Murawski, *1 Peter: A Commentary for Biblical Preaching and Teaching* (Grand Rapids: Kregel, 2022), 100.

85 E.g., Dietrich Bonhoeffer, *The Cost of Discipleship*, 1937.

subject of discipleship as the number of tree species. It's beyond the scope of this chapter to offer anything more than a few (hopefully helpful!) comments here.

First, I am encouraged by the amount of attention in our day given to the subject of discipleship (and spiritual formation/transformation) because it shows an awareness of a malady that was taking place in Christianity during the previous centuries. Three historical factors may have contributed to that malady:

- In America, both the First (eighteenth century) and Second (nineteenth century) Great Awakenings emphasized individual conversion to Christ—a wonderful blessing indeed!—but often with less emphasis on intentional living and true spiritual transformation.

- The rise of the world-wide missionary movements of the late-eighteenth and nineteenth century with their emphasis on evangelism, again focused primarily on the conversion of unbelievers (indeed, once again wonderful!).

- The rise of liberalism in the early twentieth century within the major denominations led conservatives to combat it primarily through evangelism (i.e., a conversion experience) and apologetic/polemic publications— with emphasis on knowledge more than inner spiritual transformation.

By the middle of the twentieth century, it became apparent that a large percentage of Americans (and Europeans) identified themselves as "Christians" but did not evidence an understanding of what it meant to "observe all that I have commanded you" (Matt 28:20). No doubt, gospel seeds had been planted and taken root. But relatively few saplings had fully matured and were reproducing themselves! It was time to reintroduce what a Christ-centered life meant; hence, the numerous publications on discipleship.

Second, the vast number of publications dealing with discipleship seemed to emphasize "how to" rather than "what is." Methods of disciple-making, as though discipleship were a simple process of "follow-these-five-easy-steps," appeared. Oftentimes church leaders, concerned that their members were being and making disciples, offered multi-week courses on discipleship and then encouraged their people to sign up as trained "discipleship leaders" in small group settings. Eventually, it became the norm that discipleship was only happening if your ministry held weekly small-group Bible studies, led by discipleship leaders. This method is often perpetuated today. As beneficial as these small groups may be, too often the focus rests on knowledge gained rather than life transformation.

So often we focus the vast bulk of our discipling (and evangelistic) energies on the transfer of information. And while there certainly is an unending depth to what we believe, an overemphasis on information transfer is not the most effective way to disciple others—and definitely is not the predominant biblical pattern. Several recent publications offer a better understanding of both the *what* and *how* of biblical discipleship. From one-on-one relationships to large group gatherings, from small groups and missional communities to personal time spent reading the Bible, God uses many different people and contexts to shape us into the image of Jesus Christ. When it comes to discipleship, one size does not fit all.[86]

Third, let's briefly define and clarify two important terms: *disciple* and *discipleship*. In its original ancient Greek context, the word "disciple" meant someone who was either an apprentice in a trade or a pupil of a teacher. Put another way, a disciple is someone who is learning from a master craftsman. Apprenticeship is a helpful picture for

---

86 There are more good books about discipleship than time to read them. A few highly recommended are the following: Bill Hull, *The Complete Book of Discipleship: On Being and Making Followers of Christ* (Colorado Springs: NavPress, 2006); Bobby Harrington and Alex Absalom, *Discipleship That Fits: The Five Kinds of Relationships God Uses to Help Us Grow* (Grand Rapids: Zondervan, 2016); Andrew T. Burrgraff, *Discipleship Today: Applying Biblical Discipleship in Today's Context* (Cary, NC: Shepherds Press, 2024).

it conveys the sense of a life-journey necessary for maturity. It takes time and practice to become a mature disciple, yet the only way you grow is by living out the lifestyle you are observing. Apprenticeship allows us to gain a wonderful mix of both experience and knowledge, conveyed to us in the context of a long-term, deeply committed relationship.[87] As Bobby Harrington and Alex Absalom note,

> Being a disciple means that I model my life around that of my master. I take note of how he lives, what he says, how he says it. I tease out his motivations and values so that when I encounter new situations, I can attempt to represent him faithfully. After each new experience, I discuss with him what went on and listen to his feedback, on both what went well and what could be improved next time. And then I try it out again…. As I do this, I learn to imitate what Jesus would do in the different situations and relationships of life…. In order to bear fruit as we follow Jesus, we need to grasp the centrality of discipleship as imitation.[88]

Bringing all of the above together, we can provide a definition of discipleship: *Discipleship is the process of learning the teachings of Scripture, internalizing them to shape one's belief system, and then acting upon them in one's daily life.*[89]

But what is also important to understand regarding discipleship is that God uses people to disciple us differently in various contexts; this involves more than simply what and how, but also *where* and *when*. We see this through the ways Jesus did His discipleship. There were times when Jesus impacted people through a sermon delivered to hundreds, other occasions when he was shaping a smaller,

---

87 Harrington and Absalom, *Discipleship That Fits*, 20.

88 Harrington and Absalom, *Discipleship That Fits*, 23.

89 Burggraff, *Discipleship Today*, 63.

mid-sized community of a few dozen, and other times when He was discipling His small group of twelve. And then there were those occasions when it was just Peter, James, and John. Added to these four contexts are the times when Jesus directly discipled one person without the involvement of others. When we fully grasp what Jesus did with His disciples, ranging in contexts of thousands down to one individual, we learn that God can—and does—disciple us in *every* situation of life, in *every* type of relational interaction, and that He uses *different* situations and relationships in *different* ways.[90]

If we bring this into the context of the local church, we learn how, when, and where Jesus disciples us today. Discipleship is taking place in at least five contexts:

- When the church is gathered to hear the preaching and teaching of the Word of God from the pulpit

- When groups meet in Sunday School classes or Bible Fellowship groups of dozens

- When small groups, or just a handful of people, meet to discuss, ask questions, and interact

- When one or two meet with a counsellor to deal with deeper personal issues in their Christian life

- When one is alone with God, dealing with one's struggles and issues in one's walk with God

---

90 This paragraph forms the thesis of the two books, *Discipleship That Fits* by Bobby Harrington and Alex Absalom (2016), and *Discipleship Today* by Andrew Burggraff (2024). In some ways, these two books are breakthroughs in the approach to discipleship. Of course, we should not ditch everything we've known up to now about church or small groups; rather it's time to understand that discipleship as we see in the Gospels and Acts was happening in at least *five different* relational contexts.

Therefore, we see that "the process of discipleship is done in a variety of ways and in a variety of settings in the church."[91]

Like trees in a forest in "communication" with one another, providing nutrients and protection to saplings, which may then become fruit-producing mature trees themselves, we see that God intended and then provided the means to reproduce and influence the next generation. And it's apparent God intended it to be accomplished via community. As one pastor aptly stated,

> We were not designed to do the Christian life in isolation or as an individual. So much of discipleship emphasizes the individual pursuit, and yet the New Testament again and again places the individual within the larger body of Christ that is necessary for their spiritual growth and accomplishment of God's work that he is doing to reveal himself through his people. You absolutely need one another and the connection, community, and fellowship provided by them for your spiritual growth to ultimately find and do the will of God for your life.[92]

One Generation to Another:
Investing in the Future

Like begets like (Gen 1:11, 12, 21, 24, 25), and reproduction implies *imitation*. Thus, the apostle Paul wrote to the Christians in Corinth, "Be imitators of me, as I am of Christ" (1 Cor 11:1), and "I urge you, then, be imitators of me" (1 Cor 4:16). Discipleship is *imitation*.

---

91 Burggraff, *Discipleship Today*, 63. See especially pages 63–93, where discipleship "avenues" in the local church (63–82) and one's "personal" discipleship (83–93) are discussed.

92 The quote is taken from the application made by pastor-teacher Dr. Phil Burggraff, in a sermon from 2 Sam 23, "David's Mighty Men," (Clearwater Community Church, June 15, 2025).

And he said similarly to the church at Philippi, "Brothers, join in imitating me, and keep your eyes on those who walk according to the example you have in us" (Phil 3:17 see also Phil 4:9, 1 Thess 1:6, 2 Thess 3:7). For Paul, the journey of discipleship was founded upon a lifestyle of imitation—direct imitation of Jesus as well as imitation of the lives of other believers.

Perhaps one of the clearest scriptural examples of one generation preparing another is the relationship between Paul and Timothy. It's an example of imitation and a pattern of ministry reproduction. It was noted above that Paul urged the Corinthian church "to be imitators of me" (1 Cor 4:16). He then states, "That is why I sent you Timothy, my beloved and faithful child in the Lord, to remind you of my ways in Christ, as I teach them everywhere in every church" (1 Cor 4:17). Paul does the same in his first and second letters to Timothy, addressing him as "my true child in the faith" (1 Tim 1:2) and "my beloved child" (2 Tim 1:2, 2:1, cf. Titus 1:4). Paul encourages Timothy to "Follow the pattern of the sound words that you have heard from me, in the faith and love that are in Christ Jesus" (2 Tim 1:13).

Especially important to our discussion of discipling the next generation is 2 Timothy 2:2 where Paul states, "and what you have heard from me in the presence of many witnesses entrust to faithful men, [reliable people] who will be able to teach others also." Here we see the multi-generational chain of discipleship that the Lord anticipated in Matthew 28:19–20. Therefore, "Paul demanded Timothy's active involvement in the training of a future generation of Christian servants."[93]

Paul wanted Timothy to pass gospel truths to reliable church leaders, who are trustworthy believers that are qualified to teach others. The word "faithful" teaches us that "these persons are to be 'reliable.'

---

93   Thomas D. Lea and Hayne P. Griffin, Jr., *1, 2 Timothy and Titus: The New American Commentary* (Nashville: Broadman, 1992), 200.

The word conveys integrity in matters of faith and Christian obedience. They will be faithful to what they have received, not just for their own sakes and benefit but so that they "will also be qualified to teach others."[94] Hiebert explains, "They had to be able to and competent in turn to pass on to others this treasure by their ability and willingness to teach."[95]

Paul similarly wrote Titus, another son in the faith, to instruct older believers—men and women—to assist younger believers. Just as older trees assist younger trees in their development, older believers have the responsibility to teach younger believers—older women teaching younger women and older men teaching younger men (Titus 2:2–8).

How Do We Grow the
Next Generation of Leaders?

The topic of "sowing seeds" for the purpose of reproduction of future generation begs the question, what seeds do we sow? Is there such a thing as a "leadership seed"? No. So, using trees as our metaphor is not perfect; nevertheless, there is analogy in the concept of "nurture." Trees may not shed much light on leadership (re)production, but the Word of God does, especially the Pastoral Epistles.

How does God call leaders? There can be little doubt that a great deal of confusion exists regarding the idea of a *call* to ministry. After four decades of counseling church members, college students, and seminary students, I have discovered that the average believer is unable to discuss this subject without drifting into mystical explanations. Many church members, even ministers, are unsure if there is such a thing as a call.

---

94 Yarbrough, Robert W., *The Letters to Timothy and Titus*, Pillar New Testament Commentary (Grand Rapids: Eerdmans, 2018), 372.

95 Hiebert, *Second Timothy*, 53.

What is meant by "calling"? We need to note that the term *call* or *called* in the New Testament, with reference to service or ministry, is not common. There are only a few examples (Mark 3:13–14, Acts 13:2, 16:9–10, Rom 1:1). A clear example of a distinct "call to the ministry" is seen in the life of Paul (Acts 9:1–9, 15–16). He heard the direct voice of Jesus and had a commission to "all men" (Acts 22:15). Paul knew that God had sovereignly put him into the ministry (1 Tim 1:12, 2:7, 2 Tim 1:11). He felt under divine compulsion to preach (1 Cor 9:16). This sense of compulsion was confirmed by the congregation (Acts 13:3). But does God transmit sovereign appointments today by means of such direct communication?

Direct communication from God, by definition, constitutes new revelation. Such revelation would, at least in principle, indicate that the Scriptures were not sufficient or final. Unless you believe in apostolic succession, you cannot believe the call today must come supernaturally. Today, God uses a mediated call, that is, the moving of the Holy Spirit within a person's heart that accompanies and is in agreement with the Scripture as understood and applied through proper methods of biblical interpretation. A clear example of how this happens today is found in 1 Timothy 3:1: "*This is a true saying, if a man desire the office of a bishop* [overseer]*, he desireth a good work*" (KJV).

First Timothy 3:1 refers to a man "desiring" the work of the ministry. The adjective "good" speaks of its excellence; the noun "work" speaks of its difficulty. The amount and nature of the work are seen in the title of the office labeled here as "bishop" (overseer) but has additional functions as seen in the multiple titles describing the same office elsewhere in the New Testament. The fact that it is work and demands preparation is described by Homer Kent:

> The overseership is not a mere honor to be enjoyed. Every theological student and every other aspirant to the task should note well Paul's statement. It is a good work, but it is work. One of the duties of the overseer is teaching. He

must be able to teach (v.2). To do this one task well requires serious work in preparation. And this is not his only duty.[96]

What is most important for our study are the two different verbs in 1 Timothy 3:1 that are each translated "desires." The first use of "desires" refers to "reaching out after," "to covet," "to aspire to." Of particular importance is the occurrence of this verb in the *middle voice*. The middle voice lays stress on the *agent* doing the action. In 1 Timothy 3:1, the subject is reaching after the object (i.e., the ministry) for himself—the person is causing, stirring up something within himself. He is not passively waiting for an existential, mystical call from above.

The second verb translated "desires" in 3:1 implies that the subject sets his heart upon something. The word is *epithumeo*, often translated "to love," "to desire," or "to passionately fix upon a thing." Moreover, this strong inclination of the heart can't be suppressed, even in the face of difficulty (cf. Romans 1:14–15, 15:20–21). Homer Kent writes, "This godly desire if controlled by the Spirit of God, may deepen into a sacred conviction. Such a desire is the motive for preparation in college and seminary."[97] This sheds light on the idea of a "call." The common idea has been that you shouldn't aspire to leadership in ministry—that you should wait patiently (passively) until God calls you. But that's not what the text says. To the contrary, 1 Tim. 3:1 encourages those who aspire to ministry. And that aspiration—that *desire*—needs to be "nurtured" by others.

Someone will surely ask—where is God in the call? The answer is best phrased in a question—is this desire, or divine compulsion, the direct work of the Holy Spirit? The key factor to note is this—it is the Holy Spirit who issues the call, regardless of how it comes. The call

---

96   Homer Kent, *The Pastoral Epistles* (Chicago: Moody Press, 1958), 124.

97   Kent, *The Pastoral Epistles*, 123.

may come through sheer sensitivity to God's personal dealing with us in reading the Scriptures or hearing the Word preached. More than one preacher can attest that he received his own call (deep inward desire) while sitting faithfully under the ministry of the Word.

This statement by Paul thus contradicts the all-too-common notion that a person shouldn't earnestly desire a high office of responsibility in the church. Paul says that such an aspiration is good and healthy; it should be encouraged (nurtured), not discouraged. Hence, the two key essentials relative to the "call" are:

- a desire, an abiding conviction for the work of the ministry (1 Tim 3:1)

- the biblical qualifications that speak to his spiritual character (1 Tim 3:1–7, Titus 1:5–9, 1 Peter 5:1–3)

Conclusion

Years ago, I heard Chuck Swindoll deliver a sermon on the family. He was explaining how profoundly one generation influences the next. As he spoke about child-rearing from Proverbs 22:6, he referred to the principle found in Galatians 6:7, "Do not be deceived: God is not mocked, for whatever one sows, that will he also reap," and to Proverbs 20:7, "The righteous who walks in his integrity—blessed are his children after him!" Like begets like! He used an illustration that has always stuck with me—the comparison of two families and their respective legacies. The illustration went like this:[98]

---

98 The illustration used by Chuck Swindoll was based on the research work of sociologist Richard L. Dugdale in his 1877 work *The Jukes: A Study in Crime, Pauperism, Disease and Heredity*. The comparison between the Edwards family and the Jukes family has long been used as a striking contrast between the long-term effects of virtue and vice, or of godliness versus lawlessness especially in nineteenth and early twentieth century moral and educational literature.

Two families from the 18th and 19th centuries—the Edwards and the Jukes—illustrate the long-term effects of values, education, and spiritual direction on generations. One family begins its story with a man who feared God, studied hard, served others, and led his family with biblical faith. That man was Jonathan Edwards, a prominent preacher, theologian, and president of Princeton. Edwards and his wife Sarah had 11 children. They placed a strong emphasis on education, Christian faith, and public service. Of their descendants, it is reported that they produced over 300 college graduates; over 100 pastors, missionaries, and theologians; 13 college presidents; over 60 authors; 3 U.S. Senators; 1 U.S. Vice President; and numerous doctors, judges and educators. Jonathan Edward's life-long motto was: *"Resolved, never to lose one moment of time, but improve it the most profitable way I possibly can."*

The other family began with a man marked by neglect, lawlessness, alcoholism, and moral poverty. Known only as "Max Jukes," his descendants filled prisons, brothels, and poorhouses. Among his reported descendants are 76 convicted criminals, 190 prostitutes, 60 thieves; 7 murders; over 100 lived in poorhouses; and his descendants are said to have cost the state over $1.25 million (in 19th century dollars).

The Edwards family story isn't perfect. Nor is any family's. But it teaches this: Our choices and influences ripple far beyond us.

Two men. Two legacies. One difference: the foundation—*"As for me and my house, we will serve the Lord"* (Josh 24:15).

What we sow today will be reaped tomorrow. Our influence will be seen in the next generation(s). After all, like trees, we produce "according to our kind."

BIBLIOGRAPHY

Abolfathi, Sophia. "Florida's Champion Live Oak Tree Stands Tall—A New Statewide Record-Holder in Alachua." *WUFT News,* October 4, 2023. https://www.wuft.org/human-interest/2023-10-04/floridas-champion-live-oak-tree-stands-tall-a-new-statewide-record-holder-in-alachua.

Adams, Chris. "5 Ways to Help Stressed Out Women in Your Church." *Lifeway Research,* October 30, 2014. https://www.lifewayresearch.com/2014/10/30/5-ways-to-help-stressed-out-women-in-your-church/.

Allen, David L. *Hebrews.* New American Commentary 35. Nashville: Broadman & Holman, 2010.

Arndt, William, Frederick W. Danker, Walter Bauer, and F. Wilbur Gingrich. *A Greek-English Lexicon of the New Testament and Other Early Christian Literature* 3rd ed. BDAG. Chicago: University of Chicago Press, 2000.

Barclay, William. *The Letters to Timothy, Titus, and Philemon.* Philadelphia: Westminster, 1957.

Barna Group. "Pastors Share Top Reasons They've Considered Quitting Ministry in the Past Year." https://www.barna.com/research/pastors-quitting-ministry/.

Baxter, Richard. *The Reformed Pastor.* 1656. Repr., Carlisle, PA: Banner of Truth, 1974.

Blomberg, Craig L. *1 Corinthians.* NIV Application Commentary. Grand Rapids, MI: Zondervan, 1994.

Blomberg, Craig L., and Mariam J. Kamell. *James.* Zondervan Exegetical Commentary on the New Testament 16. Grand Rapids, MI: Zondervan, 2008.

Blue, J. Ronald. "James." Pages 815–35 in *The Bible Knowledge Commentary: New Testament*. Edited by John F. Walvoord and Roy B. Zuck. Wheaton, IL: Victor Books, 1985.

Buzzell, Sid S. "Proverbs." Pages 909–66 in *The Bible Knowledge Commentary: Old Testament*. Edited by John F. Walvoord and Roy B. Zuck. Wheaton, IL: Victor Books, 1985.

Dance, Mark. "Pastors Are Not Quitting in Droves." *Lifeway Research,* July 10, 2019. https://research.lifeway.com/2019/07/10/pastors-are-not-quitting-in-droves-2/.

Davey, Stephen. *In Living Color.* Cary, NC: Charity House, 2020.

Dennehy, Kevin. "F&ES Study Reveals There Are Many More Trees Than Previously Believed." Yale School of the Environment, September 2, 2015. https://environment.yale.edu.

Dockery, David S. "The Pastor as Theologian: A Biblical Paradigm." In *The Pastor as Theologian and Scholar: Essays in Honor of John R. Ryan,* edited by David S. Dockery, 27–45. Nashville: Broadman & Holman, 2007.

Dugdale, Richard L. *The Jukes: A Study in Crime, Pauperism, Disease and Heredity.* New York: Putnam, 1877.

Geiger, Eric, and Kevin Peck. *Designed to Lead: The Church and Leadership Development.* Nashville: Broadman & Holman, 2016.

Glenn, Donald R. "Ecclesiastes." Pages 975–1007 in *The Bible Knowledge Commentary: Old Testament*. Edited by John F. Walvoord and Roy B. Zuck. Wheaton, IL: Victor Books, 1985.

Grant, Richard. "Do Trees Talk to Each Other?" *Smithsonian Magazine,* March 2018. https://www.smithsonianmag.com.

Grudem, Wayne. *Systematic Theology: An Introduction to Biblical Doctrine.* Grand Rapids, MI: Zondervan, 1994.

Henebury, Paul. "Answering the 95 Theses against Dispensationalism, Part 7." *SharperIron,* July 2010. https://sharperiron.org/article/answering-95-theses-against-dispensationalism-part-7.

Hennigan, Tom. "Talking Trees—Secrets of Plant Communication." *Answers in Genesis,* April 9, 2017. https://answersingenesis.org.

Hiebert, D. Edmond. *First Peter: An Expositional Commentary.* Chicago: Moody, 1984.

Holland, Christopher James, Michael Cole, and Jennifer Owens. "Exercise and Mental Health: A Vital Connection." *British Journal of Sports Medicine* 58, no. 13 (July 1, 2024): 691–97. https://doi.org/10.1136/bjsports-2024-108562.

Huber, Annette. "Bridegroom's Oak." *Atlas Obscura,* November 27, 2017. https://www.atlasobscura.com.

Kent, Homer. *The Pastoral Epistles.* Chicago: Moody Press, 1958.

Kittel, Gerhard, and Gerhard Friedrich, eds. *Theological Dictionary of the New Testament: Abridged in One Volume TDNTa.* Translated by Geoffrey W. Bromiley. Grand Rapids: Eerdmans, 1985.

Lea, Thomas D., and Hayne P. Griffin Jr. *1, 2 Timothy, Titus.* New American Commentary 34. Nashville: Broadman & Holman, 1992.

Luther, Martin. "Sermon to the Princes of the Empire, June 1530." In *Luther's Works,* edited by Jaroslav Pelikan, vol. 44, 289–95. Philadelphia: Fortress, 1966.

MacArthur, John. *2 Timothy.* MacArthur New Testament Commentary. Chicago: Moody Press, n.d.

———. "A Personal Glimpse: Al Sanders Interviews John MacArthur." *Grace to You,* March 8, 2001. https://www.gty.org/sermons/ GTY76/a-personal-glimpse-al-sanders-interviews-john-macarthur.

McCracken, Brett, and Ivan Mesa, eds. *Scrolling Ourselves to Death: Reclaiming Life in a Digital Age.* Wheaton, IL: Crossway, 2025.

Miller, Timothy E., and Bryan Murawski. *1 Peter: A Commentary for Biblical Preaching and Teaching.* Grand Rapids, MI: Kregel, 2022.

Mohler, R. Albert Jr. *He Is Not Silent: Preaching in a Postmodern World.* Chicago: Moody, 2008.

Mounce, William D. *Pastoral Epistles*. Word Biblical Commentary 46. Dallas: Word, 2000.

NBC News. "New Orleans' Urban Forest Survived Katrina." http://www.nbcnews.com/id/wbna9773202.

Nixon, Emily Joanne, Ellen Brooks-Pollock, and Richard Wall. "Sheep Scab Spatial Distribution: The Roles of Transmission Pathways." *Parasites & Vectors* 14 (2021): 344. https://doi.org/10.1186/s13071-021-04850-y.

Osborne, Grant R. *Matthew: Exegetical Commentary on the New Testament*. Grand Rapids, MI: Zondervan, 2010.

Piper, John. "Education about God Precedes and Serves Exultation in God." *Desiring God,* 1996. https://www.desiringgod.org.

Pittman, Thomas. "A Lifelong Learner." In *Vital Signs of a Healthy Pastor,* edited by David Deets and Richard Bargas, 59–73. Grandville, MI: IFCA International, 2025.

Rose, Reagan. "Why You're Inconsistent (And What to Do About It)." *Redeeming Productivity,* April 30, 2024. https://www.redeemingproductivity.com/why-youre-inconsistent-and-what-to-do-about-it/.

Sherwin, Frank. "Trees: An Engineering Wonder." *Institute for Creation Research,* August 31, 2015. https://www.icr.org.

Spurgeon, Charles Haddon. *Sermons Preached and Revised by C. H. Spurgeon.* Vol. 2. London: Passmore & Alabaster, 1861.

———. *The Cheque Book of the Bank of Faith: Being Precious Promises Arranged for Daily Use.* New York: American Tract Society, 1893.

Swindoll, Charles R. Sermon: "David's Mighty Men." Clearwater Community Church, June 15, 2025.

Texas A&M Forest Service. "Texas A&M Forest Service Survey Shows 301 Million Trees Killed by Drought." September 25, 2012. https://tfsweb.tamu.edu/texas-am-forest-service-survey-shows- 301-million-trees-killed-by-drought.

Towner, Philip H. *The Letters to Timothy and Titus.* New International Commentary on the New Testament. Grand Rapids, MI: Eerdmans, 2006.